You Don't Have to Eat the Eyeballs

Eyeballs

A Story of Travel,
People-Pleasing
& True Self-Love

By Katrina Bos

Cover Artist: Lynn Borth

Tellwell Talent
www.tellwell.ca

ISBN
978-0-2288-1828-1 (Paperback)
978-0-2288-1829-8 (eBook)

To my mom
Whose love continues to fill me every day.
I love you.
Thank you.

TABLE OF CONTENTS

Chapter 1   The Eyeballs on My Plate 1

SECTION I: WHY WE EAT THE EYEBALLS
Chapter 2   Defining Ourselves by Others 11
Chapter 3   It's Not Your Job To Make Anyone Happy 19
Chapter 4   The Politeness Training is Wrong........................ 29
Chapter 5   Spending Our Energy On Others 39
Chapter 6   Living in Other People's Realities.................... 53
Chapter 7   Stop Reaching So Far... or reaching at all 59

SECTION II: THE TURNING POINT
Chapter 8   Who You Are Is Important................................ 67
Chapter 9   Being My Big Beautiful Self............................ 75
Chapter 10   The Ability to Be Alone 83
Chapter 11   Being Truly Honest With Ourselves 89
Chapter 12   Your Truth Always Matters........................... 99
Chapter 13   Following Our Inner Truth 109

SECTION III: FINDING TRUE SELF-LOVE
Chapter 14   True Self-Love.. 115
Chapter 15   Sometimes You Must Leave........................... 121
Chapter 16   Going Home... 127

Acknowledgements.. 129
About the Author.. 131

CHAPTER 1

THE EYEBALLS ON MY PLATE

Oh my god, they want me to eat the eyeballs.

The fish eyeballs looking up at me on the plate were nearly as big as mine. What had I gotten myself into? Why had I agreed to come to this island? Had I taken a wrong turn? Had my intuition been off with this one?

"Ummm... I've never eaten eyeballs before."

"Oh, they are the best part. They are delicious. You must eat them," my new friend replied.

She said this with a thick French/Creole accent. I was staying with her on the island to help her improve her English for two months. This was just day two and I already felt like I was failing her. She was so excited to share her culture with me and I was already disappointing her. I was feeling like a very ungrateful guest.

"Watch me," she said, reaching across the table to steal one of the eyeballs from her husband's plate, demonstrating that eating eyeballs is totally normal.

Surprisingly, her husband pushed her fork away. It was very obvious that he wasn't sharing his eyeballs with anyone.

Hmmm... he must really like them. Darn.

She proceeded to stab one of the eyeballs on *my* plate, plunk it into her mouth and say, "See! It's delicious! You *must* try it!"

A million thoughts raced through my mind. *She ate the eyeball. She didn't die. I am here to have new experiences, and expand what is possible. People must eat these all of the time here. Maybe they're good for you. Her husband loves them. And besides, I eat weiners. We all know that there are worse ingredients than eyeballs in them!!*

Well, that one stuck. This became my eyeball-eating-mantra. *You eat weiners Katrina. Just put the eyeball in your mouth. It's no worse than a weiner.* I repeated this over and over until I finally picked up my fork, took a deep breath in and stabbed the little sucker.

OK. This was already gross. Stabbing eyeballs with a fork was just so wrong. Maybe I had watched too many horror movies as a child but this just felt wrong on so many levels.

Now, however, it was on the fork. I continued my mantra: *You eat weiners Katrina. You eat weiners Katrina. You've done harder things. This is nothing. You can do this!*

And the eyeball went into my mouth.

Well, whatever you think it feels like to have a big eyeball rolling around in your mouth, you are 100% right! It's kind of firm, soft, slimy and it was completely freaking me out.

Then, I had the horrible realization that it was too big to swallow whole. I was going to have to bite the eyeball in half. This was just getting worse.

Just bite and swallow, I told myself. Just make it happen. You're 49 years old! You can do this. You've done harder things. Just chew and swallow. You can do this!!

And so I bit down only to find something hard and crunchy in the middle of it!! *OMG OMG OMG!!*

I instantly spit it out onto my plate with a bit of a squeal. My hosts laughed for a moment and then asked, "What is wrong?"

"THERE'S SOMETHING HARD IN THE MIDDLE!!" I sputtered.

"Yes, you just crunch it. It is good."

Well, that was it. I was finished. My gag reflexes had totally taken over and there was no way anything was entering my mouth for a long time.

I felt horrible. Before I had arrived on the island, my hostess had sent me pictures of all amazing seafood dishes, waterfalls, and beautiful dancers in bright, vivid costumes - all the amazing aspects of her culture. I knew that sharing this eyeball experience meant a lot to her. And here I was, literally spitting out the eyeballs.

Staring at the partially chewed eyeball on my plate, I felt an incredible mix of emotions. Part of me was really proud that I had even put it into my mouth. I tend to be a pretty simple eater - a "meat and potatoes" kind of girl. Trying to eat an eyeball was a pretty big step for me. But I was still pretty sad to have disappointed her.

I was in a new phase in life. I was seeking authentic experiences and I was open to being uncomfortable so that I could grow into new parts of myself. So, perhaps, this experience made sense. It was uncomfortable and I never could have imagined it.

But eyeballs? Really? I'm not sure that this was what I was seeking.

I guess we would see.

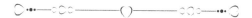

RECOGNIZING THE EYEBALLS OF LIFE

I was sitting in a café writing this book when an old friend came in. She was a woman whom I had loved and respected for decades. In her thirties, she had been independent in a time when most of us were married, struggling and really needing to be attached to someone. She had always seemed to have it all together... until about 8 years ago, when she fell in love, got married and had a baby.

Now, there are obviously lovely parts of this chapter of her story. But what I noticed each time I saw her since getting married, was that she seemed a little more tired and beaten down. Her husband was a strong personality like her and they were really struggling as a couple. She was trying to be a "good" wife. She was trying to be considerate. She was listening to her husband's thoughts. She was compromising. But so far, they had spent most of their marriage in counselling trying to get to the bottom of why they were having so many problems.

On this day, in the café, she asked me what I was writing about. I told her the eyeballs story and how many of us are metaphorically eating the eyeballs all of the time. How we do things that we don't want to do for a hundred reasons. Sometimes just to make other people happy. Sometimes out of obligation. And sometimes it's just what we learned as children. But regardless, once we realize we are doing it, we start noticing "eyeballs" everywhere in our lives.

At this point, my friend got this sad look on her face, looked down at the ground and said, "I think that every single thing I'm doing today is an eyeball."

This really struck me because I had always admired this woman. She was my "goddess friend". It made sense that I, who had always struggled with low self-esteem, might choose to eat the eyeballs to make other people happy. But my goddess-friend? I knew I was really onto something.

FROM PEOPLE-PLEASING TO SELF-LOVE

I have always been a people-pleaser. The desires and needs of others have always come first for me - even as a child. I wanted to please my parents, grand-parents and teachers. I wanted my friends' parents to like me. I wanted other kids to like me. So, I tended to go along with the crowd, not rocking the boat, trying not to stand out in "unpopular" ways.

It is only recently, in the travels described in this book, that I discovered that self-love is the only path that actually makes me happy. Previously, the concept of self-love brought to mind visions of long baths, stating your needs to your partner, and staring into the mirror telling yourself that you were pretty and loved and a worthy person.

These things never appealed to me. No matter how many baths I took or how many times I told myself that I was awesome, lovable and perfect just the way I was, there was absolutely no impact on my self-worth or happiness.

However, a year ago, things started changing for me. I was newly single, my children were grown and moving on with their lives and it was time for a new chapter in my life. I had always had a vision of travelling the world with nothing but a backpack. And the time had now come to make that vision a reality.

So, in November 2018, I gave away all of my belongings, furniture, household items, sold my car to my son, and hopped on a plane to Europe with my backpack and my computer. I would follow my inner calling and go wherever felt right. I had no official plan except that my first stop would be Ireland where my daughter was living with her girlfriend. This was a pretty safe spot to start.

I had found an interesting website called talktalkbnb.com where people invite you into their homes so that they can practise whatever new language they are learning. In my case, people invited me to stay with them to improve their English. In return I would get room and board and become part of their family. It's a fabulous program which I highly recommend. It gave me a beautiful balance between having the freedom of a tourist and getting to experience really being part of a family and therefore fully immersed in a culture. It is quite an amazing opportunity.

However, there was also a darker side to this opportunity which, as difficult as it was at times, created opportunities for incredible growth inside of me. And it isn't that the people I stayed with were mean or treated me badly. They simply became characters in my own personal drama. Their different cultures and living within their families, definitely pushed my emotional buttons. Whatever unresolved issues were hiding within me were brought to the surface - resulting in many "aha" moments and the most incredible breakthrough - finally being able to treat myself with the same kind of love that I had given to others my whole life.

And I'm not talking about the "stand in front of the mirror and smile" kind of self-love. I'm talking about a true and genuine connection to my inner self, "my little girl", and my deepest truth. Bit by bit, all of the ideas, trainings and beliefs that had always caused me to sacrifice my deepest happiness for the sake of others were disappearing.

One thing that helped speed up this process was nearly always being in a state of discomfort. When you are literally carrying everything you own in a backpack and you are not surrounded with your comfort foods, your favourite chair, or your friends and family, it is pretty easy to be a little more on edge. Plus, I was often in a country where, although I had studied the language a little bit, I normally had no idea what was being said most of the time.

The combination of all of these things kept me in a constant state of unknown. This may sound like a negative thing, but it became a key player in my growth and expansion. We are often taught that the goal of life is to create such comfort and reliable expectations, that a large part of us ends up dying - becoming stagnant in the very water that we have worked so hard to keep still.

Living on my emotional edge like this forced me to go a little bit deeper and observe the situation more carefully. And it wasn't always pretty. Sometimes I broke down in tears. Sometimes I spent weeks feeling lost and confused. Sometimes, after being with a group of people and not having understood a word anyone said for over 12 hours, I truly questioned my sanity and emotional well-being.

It is often said that after the darkest night, the sun rises and things are brighter than ever.

This is my story.

WHY WE EAT THE EYEBALLS

Chapter 2

Defining Ourselves by Others

I had been asked to come to the island to help my hostess with her English. I was given my own bedroom and bathroom. Everything was really nice. The only thing they mentioned that might be an inconvenience was that the town was working on the water pipes so that we would only have running water for half of the day. We wouldn't necessarily know which half - either morning or night. But the water would only be there sometimes and sometimes not for days.

Well, my hosts worked very long hours. They would leave by 7 a.m. every morning and not get home until 7 p.m. at night. The water was often on during the day when they were at work. By the time they got home at night, it had been turned off. So, the dishes from dinner would pile up in the kitchen. Laundry was piling up in the bathrooms. They simply weren't home when the water was on. It was impossible for them to get these chores done.

Well their long days at work gave me wonderful time to write, do web design, and create videos and online courses. Once the water came on in the morning, it would be easy for me to do the dishes and do a load of laundry or two each day to help them get caught up.

So I did. Every day, I would do the dishes and clean the kitchen. I would put a load of laundry in the washer, hang it out to dry, and fold it into piles for them.

On the first day that I did this, I was so happy to be able to contribute in this small way. I really appreciated getting to stay with them and I wanted to help out. I was part of their family and I wanted to create a connection. After all, I was a stranger. I wanted them to know I was willing to pitch in and be a part of things.

But when they came home that night, they walked by the folded laundry without so much as a look and went into the kitchen to start making supper... without saying a word to me.

Now, it could be that I am Canadian (we are known to be polite to a fault). It could be that I personally would have thanked someone for doing that. I don't know. But I was kind of shocked that they didn't say anything. But that was okay. They were tired after a long day's work. It was no big deal. I shouldn't need verbal appreciation anyway. I'm a big girl.

The next day, it was the same. The water was only on during the day so I did the dishes, the laundry, and my own work and felt really happy that I could help out again.

When they came home... the same... nothing.

This continued day after day. And each day, I would go through this exhausting internal dialogue. *Oh Katrina, relax. They are just tired. They appreciate it. They just don't say it in this culture. It's nothing personal.*

But what if I'm wrong? What if they are mad at me? What if they're insulted? Maybe they think it's rude to do their laundry. I had asked and she said that it was okay but maybe she didn't actually want me to do it. Maybe they think I'm not being a good guest and accepting their hospitality by "working" for them during the day. Maybe they don't like the way I stack the dishes or fold the laundry.

My inner dialogue was absolutely exhausting.

On the fifth day, I knew that they were taking me away on the weekend on adventures around the island. I figured that they would definitely never get ahead of that laundry and so I thought I would really help out and do three loads of laundry. There were some blankets filling the laundry bins. Getting them out of the way would really help out. (Honestly, sometimes I still think like I'm a farm-wife and mother.)

But what if it makes them mad? What if they don't thank me and I get even more upset?

Then I realized that I would do this for anyone. If I was in any of my friend's houses, I would pitch in. I would help out. It wasn't even out of obligation. I would simply do it because it was a nice thing to do.

After much inner battle, my inner mantra became "Just be you. You don't have to understand them or what they're thinking".

So, I chose to be me. That night, when they got home, the kitchen was clean and all the laundry was done.

My hostess walked in and looked at the chair with the folded blankets on it, looked at me and said, "It was sunny today?"

"Yes. It was beautiful."

She just "humphed" and walked away.

I sat there partially confused and a little entertained. I had learned something about myself. I learned that I was going to be me no matter what. And I learned that I would continue being me whether there was appreciation or not.

This was a really big deal as a people-pleaser. It was good to know that I would have done it regardless. That it wasn't just to win her favour. That it is just who I was regardless of the effects on others.

Now, I'm not saying that I enjoyed the situation at all. I didn't. And although I did continue to help out, I never once got an indication of whether what I was doing was okay or not - whether it was appreciated or whether it was offensive. And I doubt I will ever know.

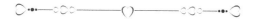

THE DANGEROUS
REFLECTION OF OTHERS

The reality is that we are social creatures. We learn about who we are by what other people reflect back to us. There *are* people who are immune to these reflections and are truly self-defined - but they are rare. Most of us base a lot of what we understand about ourselves on the reactions of those around us.

Just imagine how early this starts. By no fault of our parents, they give birth to us exactly as they are at that point in time. Who they are and their sense of self-worth has been formed by their experiences up until that point.

As we're growing up, if we have qualities that our parents respect, we may be praised. If we have qualities that they don't like, we may be criticized. If we are raised in a family that believes that higher education and a financially lucrative career are the only sign of success, then each child within that family will define themselves either as a successful person, or not, based on this scale of judgement.

If we are raised in a culture and family who believes that women are meant to be subservient and are less than men, then we will either adopt this belief or we will fight against it and believe ourselves to be a rebel and a problem. However, this same "problem child" in a different family, that believed in equality, would not have this definition and continue on in life believing that they were easy to get along with.

Even our definition of beauty and self-esteem is highly subjective based on our cultures. There are cultures where only thinness and athleticism are prized as true beauty. Then there are others where curves and big bottoms signify wealth, status and sensual desire.

Our education system may define whether we believe we are intelligent or not. If the system fits your learning style and you give the right answers, you may believe you are an intelligent person. If you don't give the right answers or your way of learning or thinking is not the same as the system, then you may believe that you are unintelligent and therefore will never succeed.

Later in life, this may also happen at work. In a work environment, what others think of us can impact our success and promotion opportunities. So, our focus on how others see us intensifies further.

THE BROKEN REFLECTION OF OTHERS

It is not only the reflection from our culture that we internalize, it is also all of the people who we are closest to. Every word spoken and look given to us can alter our perception of self. If we feel a close bond with our parents, this sends a message to us that we are lovable. If we don't have a healthy connection with our parents, we can spend our lives feeling abandoned and defensive so we will not be hurt again in such a deep way.

We can imagine the people around us literally like mirrors. The accuracy of the reflection will depend on the wholeness of the mirror. If the mirror is in pristine condition, we may actually get an accurate reflection back. This happens with others who are very self-aware. They might have been through difficulties in life, have learned a lot, and hold great wisdom. Sometimes, they are simply very humble and unassuming.

We always know when we have met someone who is a "clear mirror" because we learn something about ourselves that neither builds up our ego nor makes us feel badly about ourselves. They simply reflect the truth about who we are. We actually get to see who we are just by looking into their eyes.

However, more often than not, the people surrounding us are quite broken mirrors themselves. They have so many personal issues, hang-ups, painful history, and insecurities that they cannot reflect a pure image. To internalize any reflection from these people can be very dangerous to our self-worth.

Yet, we know no different. We may have been surrounded by broken mirrors for our whole life. It is all we know. It begins when we are children. Our tapestry gets woven without our input, without our awareness or consciousness. What others think, what they desire, what they value - it all becomes the tapestry of who we believe that we are.

Our Soul's Tipping Point

We live like this for a time. We will unconsciously believe that who we are and our perception of reality is accurate because it is all we have ever known.

And then *something* happens. Maybe we are diagnosed with a disease. Maybe our marriage breaks up. Or we suffer from depression. Maybe we find ourselves broke and without hope for the future. Or we just feel empty inside and without meaning.

The path that we have taken based on the tapestry created by our childhood didn't take us where it promised. We were supposed to be happy and successful but it didn't happen. Our marriage ended. We got sick. We didn't like the life that we had created at all.

At this point, our soul begs to be heard again. It starts crying out to be brought back into our lives.

We start to question ourselves. What do we really love to do in life? Is our definition of self accurate? Have we been giving ourselves the short end of the stick thus far?

What is our truth about various situations in our lives? Why have we not been listening? Why did our truth and perspective not matter? Why is our sadness and frustration not important?

If we are lucky, we begin a journey of finding ourselves. This idea might seem simple and unimportant, but it really isn't. Without our core self, who are we really? Why are we even bothering to walk through our days, if it isn't *our true selves* doing the walking? To simply allow the robotic parts of us complete our tasks day after day is not really an accomplishment.

Perhaps this journey to our soul is more important than we think.

WHAT MIRRORS ARE WE CHOOSING?

It is also interesting to look at the mirrors that we choose to see ourselves in.

I had a really difficult time emotionally in high school and I think part of the reason is that I chose the popular kids to be my mirror. It was my reflection in *their* eyes that defined me as a person. If *they* liked me, then I was likeable. If *they* invited me out, then I was important. If *they* liked my new jeans, then I was cool.

But it didn't work. They weren't interested in me. I had nothing that they wanted.

In hindsight, I have realized that the other 90% of the students would have been wonderful mirrors for me that could have reflected a version of myself that I loved and respected. Later, at high school reunions, people would tell how much they had respected how smart I was. Lovely men told me that they had crushes on me and I had no idea. I had been so focused on the wrong people that I didn't see anyone else.

I've often done this in my adult life as well. I laugh at myself now when I think of how often I was worried about what other people were thinking about me. If I walked down a beach, what if people thought I was fat? Or what if someone didn't like something that I was wearing?

These were complete strangers!

When I first became single in my forties, I became hyper-focused on what my body looked like and any signs of ageing. It didn't stop me from dating but I did notice how focused I was on it.

But then I would remember that the men who had truly loved me saw me for who I was. They loved every inch of me and never noticed if I gained or lost weight (or got a hair-cut for that matter). They just loved me. Period.

CHAPTER 3

IT'S NOT YOUR JOB TO MAKE ANYONE HAPPY

Some of us are born with "servant's hearts". We love helping others. But, sometimes in our desire to help and fix others, we end up eating a lot of eyeballs. We do things because we *should*. We do things because the other person is suffering. How could we not help?

In 1999, I experienced a healing journey which I write about in my book *What If You Could Skip the Cancer?*. I come from a long line of women who have died of cancer. So, when I found lumps growing in my breast, I needed to find another way. As serendipity would have it, a teacher appeared in my life just at the perfect time. Not only did I heal physically, I had begun my deeper spiritual journey of listening within for guidance and becoming who I truly was

After a bit of time had passed and I was all better, I called this man (my teacher) and asked him if he would teach me how to heal others like he did. I wanted to help people. There were so many people who were sick and struggling. "This is what I really want to do with my life," I said.

He replied, "Katrina, why in the world would you want to do that?"

What? How could he say that? Who wouldn't want to be a healer? I didn't understand.

He continued, "Katrina, I think you should go away and think about why you would ever want to do something like this."

Well, completely confused, I went away and thought about it.

After a while, I realized that I wanted to heal people because I wasn't comfortable with their unhappiness. I wanted to fix them. I wanted to make them better. But then I realized that each of us has to find our *own* happiness. It wasn't up to anyone else to make us happy. This was actually impossible.

I had to imagine just letting other people be themselves; allow them to thrive, suffer, struggle or be happy. I had to deeply understand that other people's happiness had absolutely nothing to do with me.

I realized that this desire to make others happy had seriously contributed to my depression over the years because I would constantly be doing things that I really didn't want to do. I did them in the name of love. I did them because I thought others wanted me to. I did them because it was easier than being around people who were grumpy and unhappy.

I really had to ask myself why I was really doing it and recognize that on some level, it definitely wasn't making *me* happy at all.

PEOPLE-PLEASING VS BEING GIVING

I had always thought that making people happy was part of being a kind and giving person. I figured that it was just the right way to be.

I learned there is a big difference between being a people-pleaser (eating eyeballs) and being a giving person. In fact, being a people-pleaser really wasn't a good idea. Why should our goal be to make someone *else* happy? Why wasn't it *their* goal to make themselves happy? Why weren't *they* the ones who were responsible for that?

To be honest, when I imagined not being a people-pleaser, I felt a fear rise up in me. Would this mean that I was no longer going to be a nice person? Was I now going to *not please* others. If I were no longer a people-*pleaser*, would I become a people-*displeaser*?

I had no desire to displease others or rebel against anything. This just wasn't my nature.

This is where the problem lies.

There is a big difference between risking disappointing someone by being honest and being rebellious. When we are rebelling, we do everything in our power to do the opposite of what would make another person happy. Our primary goal is to displease the other which normally either causes more problems or makes a difficult relationship even worse.

This is not what we are talking about.

We are talking about simply living according to our own truth, following our own path whether others are pleased or not, actually getting to live our own lives.

WHERE DOES PEOPLE-PLEASING COME FROM?

Personally, as soon as I met my husband, it was like a spell came over me. From that moment on, all I wanted to do was make him happy. I became hyper-focused on his emotional state. How was he today? Was he happy with me? Was he okay?

It went further. Were his parents happy with me? Did they think I was a good wife to their son? Did they approve of me?

As I write this, it seems like so long ago and these are thoughts that I can't even imagine thinking today. But that was how it was. On many topics, I stood my ground and it didn't matter what others thought of me. When it came to raising our children, I was absolute in what I knew was right. When it came to religion, health or philosophies of life, I was also pretty opinionated.

However, there was a very specific channel where my husband ruled. On this channel, I couldn't think straight if there was distance between us. My desire for him to be happy was far more important than my own happiness. If he was upset about something, I would change my behaviour, cook his favourite meal, help him more in the barn - basically anything I could do to make things better.

So perhaps it makes sense that it was so difficult to leave the marriage after 20 years. On the one hand, I really believed in marriage. I am a romantic and I loved the idea of being married. But on the other hand, there was an invisible thread that made my husband's opinions, perspective, and version of reality more important than mine.

The road out became a series of awakenings where I realized that, for some reason, only his feelings seemed to matter and mine didn't. I realized that I was consciously and unconsciously responding to every emotion of his. I realized that I would walk on eggshells if it meant that he would be happy.

The amazing thing was that once I decided that it was time to leave, it was like a spell had lifted. I couldn't believe that I had ever thought those thoughts. I couldn't understand why I hadn't seen the situation clearly before. It was so strange.

Today, I find it very different listening to people who are married and "happy-ish". I listen to how they *have* to do this, how they hate it when their spouse does *that*, how they just put up with it because "what else can they do".

I watch spouses yell at each other. I see them be incredibly unkind to one another. In this moment, I am sitting in Greece where some people still believe that men are superior to women. I watch the men snap their fingers and expect the women to do their bidding. Most of the time, the women argue about it but eventually are worn down and they do what their husband wants in order to keep the peace or because it's just easier than fighting.

I observe it but it is like watching a TV show where the characters are bewitched in some way. They have lost their sense of self. They think that all of this anger and distrust is normal. They are interacting with someone who doesn't treat them with respect or even love.

Then, to top it all off, not only do they put up with the behaviour and meanness, they also believe that it is their job to make sure that their partner is happy.

Why would we think it's up to us to make our partner happy, regardless of how they treat us?

People-Pleasing as a Survival Mechanism

We do it because there was a time when our lives depended on it.

A hundred years ago, in most parts of the world, women could not work, vote and didn't have the same human rights as men. Therefore, keeping the man of the house happy was a requirement for survival. Plus, birth control didn't exist. Therefore, there were normally also children to consider. If a woman did not please her husband, she could be discarded and she and her children would be without food and shelter.

And it certainly isn't just women. Maybe in our ancestry, we were slaves or servants. Pleasing the boss meant avoiding punishment and sheer survival for ourselves and our family.

In our modern lives, pleasing our parents might have meant getting candy, getting to go out with our friends, or getting new shoes. In school, we learned how to get good grades by impressing our teachers. As adults, we learn how to keep difficult bosses happy in order to simply pay the bills. This survival mechanism has been very important to keep a roof over our heads and food on the table.

Becoming a Parent

If I had been overly focused on others before having children, becoming a mother took it to a whole new level. Once I got pregnant, it was as if I was being trained moment by moment that my life was no longer my own.

I was sick every day of both of my pregnancies. Pre-pregnancy, I would go to my job as a computer programmer, talk to people, eat lunch, write code, and drive home. But once I was pregnant, I would wake up, be sick to my stomach, drive to work, feel nauseous all day and try to hold it together just to get the work done. Then I would be sick on the way home (I couldn't stand any motion) all the while getting thinner and thinner while my baby grew inside of me.

No matter how abstract we want to be about this, literally having another human inside your body changes your consciousness. My body was changing moment to moment to accommodate this new life. Each day of those nine months prepared me for considering and caring for another human - 24 hours a day.

And then my baby was born. From that day forward, I was aware of another person every moment of the day. Even when he was sleeping, some part of me was listening for a cry, sensing if anything was wrong, and being constantly ready in case he woke up.

They say that if you want something to become natural so that you can do it without thinking, then you must do it consistently every day. Well, having a child trains you every moment of the day to be aware of another person. And this training goes on for decades which is certainly long enough to end up being completely reprogrammed and having totally forgotten what it was like to only consider yourself before this massive change happened.

For some women, going to work gives them a chance to still remember who they are outside of being a mother. However, the children are still always on their mind. Whether it is a phone call from school or a sick child in the morning, they are perpetually connected to their children's emotional well-being. This training to always be aware of others becomes very deep and well-rooted.

CARING FOR PARENTS

We can also develop this habit as children, if our parents are sick or really demanding.

When we are raised with a parent who has an illness and needs constant care, we learn at a young age to keep one ear open always listening for them. Are they okay? Do they need any help?

If a parent is depressed or has mental health challenges, all we want is for them to be happy. Our parents are essentially gods to us for many years. We love them more than anyone. So, it's very natural for us to be totally focused on them. A certain part of our consciousness becomes attached to their moment-to-moment well-being.

This training is not easy to let go of. It is subconsciously stored away. And we don't even know that it's been hardwired inside of us.

BEING THE "BECK-AND-CALL" GIRL

And then there was married life on the farm.

My husband's name was Wayne. I used to call myself "Wayne's beck-and-call-girl". I would literally have just begun working on something in the house and I would hear a yell from the barn "KAAAAAATTTTT! Can you come help?!"

And he always genuinely needed me. The cows might have gotten out and he needed help rounding them up. Or a feeder had broken and fixing it required more than two hands. It wasn't like I could ask him to wait a couple hours for me to finish what I was doing. On a farm, things break, accidents happen, animals do crazy things and everything has to be attended to immediately.

Well, it didn't take too long for me to stop even starting my own projects. I soon learned that I would never get to finish them. Not only would I likely be interrupted, there were always cows to milk, fields to plant, frozen water pipes to fix. You just got used to fighting whatever fire was burning brightest.

To this day, I still struggle with just focusing on my own work and interests - especially when surrounded by others. It's like whatever everyone else is doing is always more important than whatever I want to do.

It could even be checking my email while I'm working on something else - always scanning for the needs of others. Of course, it is often easier to answer someone else's question or solve their problems than to dig deep within and continue in my creativity.

And these are just a few examples. As I notice all the places that I focus on others first, I realize that I do it in nearly every aspect of my life.

CHAPTER 4

THE POLITENESS TRAINING IS WRONG

Then there are the things we do (but don't want to) because we have to be "polite". Over time, this need/requirement to be polite can cause an awful lot of eyeball-eating.

When my daughter was little, I discovered that she had been wetting her pants every day at school. She was horribly embarrassed and hid it from me for a long time. But eventually, I found out. (She, of course, is thrilled that I'm now sharing this publicly.)

When I asked her what was going on, she said that she would tell me but I had to promise not to say anything to her teacher. I agreed and she shared that her teacher wasn't letting them go to the bathroom. That when they asked to go, he would yell and scream and say something to shame them like, "What are you guys, a bunch of babies?" Or "Maybe you should go back to kindergarten!" They were seven years old.

To avoid his anger and taunting, the children eventually just stopped asking.

At this point, I was definitely regretting promising that I wouldn't say anything. But my daughter was afraid that things would just get worse. So, reluctantly, I kept my promise.

Luckily, a few days later, we had parent-teacher interviews. I would have a chance to get a sense of this guy myself. As we sat there with him, he spoke about all of the normal things - report cards and how our daughter was doing - and then I tried to say something without betraying my promise to my daughter.

I said, "Are you aware that many of the children are afraid of you?"

He looked at me for a moment, took a deep breath, became quite cocky and said, "Oh I think your daughter is just afraid of men. That's all."

I looked at him for a moment and let that sink in. The truth was that my daughter wasn't afraid of anything or anyone. She was the most confident little girl that I knew (and still is). But this man's eyes and attitude told me the whole story. I didn't need to know any more from him.

When we got home, my daughter was sitting waiting for us.

"So what happened? You didn't say anything did you?"

I replied, "Here's what you need to understand sweetie. Some people are just assholes (I didn't normally talk like this, so it was kind of shocking). Your teacher only has two jobs to do. He must teach you and he must keep you safe. These are his only responsibilities. The reality is that he is being rude to you. He's disrespecting you. And just because he is an adult and in a position of authority does not mean that you have to do everything he says. He is not allowed to treat you like this. Period."

I continued, "From here on in, if he is rude to you or doesn't let you go to the bathroom, I want you to stand up and simply start walking out of the room. If he asks you where you are going or yells at you, I want you to calmly take a piece of paper, write down my name and our home phone number and give it to him. You can tell him that he can talk to your Mom about it."

Amazingly, she never had another problem. She never had to get up and leave. Everything was fine. Ironically, at the end of the year, enough parents had complained about him that he was sent on some kind of anger management training and when he returned the following year he had transformed and ended up being one of the most beloved teachers.

THE POLITE EYEBALLS

I was raised to be very polite. My grandfather and uncle were both ministers. Because my grandfather was a chaplain in the Air Force, my dad and his family often lived on AirForce bases so the military correctness training was also there. My parents were teachers. We did things "right".

Some of the training was healthy and nice: no elbows on the table, no hats in the house, don't interrupt others, ask to leave the table, things like that.

My parents were also fun and approachable. It wasn't all perfect manners and no slouching. But on occasion, we would get together with grandma and grandpa, my dad's brother and sister, and all the cousins. *Those* dinners were a whole other story.

Everyone had to be dressed properly, sitting straight, not playing with anything, not interrupting the adults, and using the proper fork and spoon. For us kids, it was somewhere between the entertainment of "eating dinner at the queen's" and it being pure torture. First, there was the novelty of the fancy plates, cutlery and the fact that we got real wine glasses. That's fun for a bit. Then the food would come and it would be delicious. It was after this that our politeness training would be put to the test.

As everyone was finishing their meals, the adults would start to talk... and not about interesting things to us children. We obviously weren't contributing to the conversation at all. We were "to be seen and not heard". So we sat there, shifting in our seats, trying not to fall over from sheer boredom. We would play with the wine glasses, wetting the rim and running our fingers around them to make them sing - until we were told not to. We would breathe onto our spoons and hang them on our noses - until we were told not to. There was absolutely nothing to do. So, we either acted up and got in trouble or we just sat there like zombies.

SO WHY IS THIS EXPECTED?

Politeness wasn't just created to torture young people. There were good reasons for each rule.

For example, let's say that someone is always dominating a conversation with topics about themselves or about something that no one else is interested in. Perhaps they interrupt others when they are speaking. It would be good for these people to be told to "Just listen. Even if you're not interested or it is difficult to control yourself, just sit and listen for a little while. It's polite."

Learning how to listen politely as a child and therefore learning that other people have interesting things to say and interesting perspectives is a very valuable teaching. This definitely serves us well in life.

And most of the time, this is nice. It's good to listen to your grandparents when they are forgetting that they have already told you a story 20 times. They took care of us when we were little. We can be respectful, polite, and listen to them for a little while.

However, in the wrong circumstances, it can also be incredibly painful. It may sound like an overstatement to say "pain" but pretending is actually quite exhausting and if it goes on for too long, a real despair can set in - a complete lack of enjoyment and lack of meaning in life.

If this is a pattern in a marriage or a job or a culture where you must simply sit quietly, listen, and act appropriately, something eventually dies inside. It's easy to forget who we are. We stop forming opinions. We stop genuinely interacting with the people around us. We essentially become zombies.

Very polite and depressed zombies.

HIDING THE INAPPROPRIATE BEHAVIOUR OF OTHERS

This politeness training pops up in all kinds of different places.

A good friend of mine is a successful business woman in her 40s. She's happily single, independent and strong.

One night she found herself at a party. She was having a great time until she was playing pool and a man (who was there with his wife) came up behind her and ran his hands over her bottom. She didn't know anyone else at the party and was feeling quite vulnerable. So she just stared at him with a look that said, "What are you doing?"

He just smiled back and continued to touch her, then winked and walked on.

She snapped out of whatever deer-in-the-headlights state she was in and went into the other room and asked another woman if she had seen what had happened. Was she imagining it? Did that guy actually just feel her up?

For the rest of the night, she avoided him and his wife but she was definitely no longer having any fun.

The next day, she called me and told me the story. Her big question was "Why didn't I say anything? Why did I just let him touch me? Whether he was married or not, why didn't I tell him to keep his hands to himself? I absolutely didn't want him to touch me in any way. Why didn't I say something?"

The challenge is that there is an unsaid rule that said that she should be *polite* about it and that she shouldn't cause a stir. That she shouldn't cause unnecessary attention or negativity. That somehow if she said something, that *she* would be the one causing trouble.

Now don't get me wrong. There are a lot of times that we absolutely stand up for ourselves and don't allow this kind of behaviour - even *this* woman had stood up for herself many times in this kind of situation in the past.

But what's interesting is that there are still times that we don't. That there are still some instances where this old programming inside wins and we keep quiet. They will go away. Don't cause a stir. Don't cause a problem.

TOLERATING BAD BEHAVIOUR

If someone else knows that your politeness training will keep you in check, they may feel free to say all kinds of inappropriate things. I have had people say sexist, sexual and degrading things to me over the years knowing that I will stay silent, leaving me furious as to why I didn't say anything. Why didn't I stand up for myself?

It could also be a family gathering where everyone knows that we will be on our best behaviour because we only get together on special occasions a couple of times a year. Unfortunately, this is often where people will get in their best "jabs" (adding alcohol often makes this even worse).

These jabs might be subtle, passive-aggressive insults waged across the room. It might be something said in a private conversation. It might be a sarcastic remark at the dinner table. The key is that the sender of the remark knows that no one will say anything "because it's Christmas". And if the recipient dared say anything back, the resulting comments would be "Oh for God's sake, why are you causing trouble? It's Christmas. They didn't mean it! They're just kidding around."

This can also happen in marriages. When we believe in "till death do you part" and that marriage is about accepting the good with the bad, this can set us up for some very rough times depending on the relationship.

For example, what if one partner is particularly badly behaved? They might be emotionally, verbally or physically abusive. Maybe they are sarcastic. Maybe they do things that bother the other person like drink too much, go out with their friends all the time, don't share in the child-rearing, or even have affairs. If the other person's politeness training goes deep enough, they might "take the high road" and tell themselves that it's all okay.

They will try to change *themselves* to make things alright. They might assume that *they* have done something wrong to cause this behaviour and therefore turn the other cheek. Or, like in the Christmas dinner example, they may simply stay quiet because they don't want to rock the boat or cause trouble.

TAKING THE HIGH ROAD

But what if this isn't the high road at all? What if the high road is actually being honest? What if the best thing we can do for everyone is to call attention to the behaviour in the kindest way possible and address what is truly going on?

Tolerating repeated bad behaviour isn't polite. It is being a doormat. It is having no say. It is not believing that you have the right to an opinion or that your perception of the situation isn't valid.

There is obviously a time to "be the bigger person" if someone is being rude or obnoxious. It is often a healthy thing to not stoop to their level and maintain kindness and a clear mind instead of being reactionary and saying or doing something we might regret later. It's good to take a breath and understand that the other person is upset, overly emotional, angry, grieving, etc and might actually regret their current actions later. Having a cool head about it will definitely help maintain a positive relationship in the long run.

However, this can definitely be abused when one person knows that the other won't say anything and this bad behaviour can continue for many, many years.

WHEN TO BE POLITE

Politeness in its purest form simply asks us to be kind and considerate to others. There is no reason to get rid of it. It's a lovely way to be.

Once in a while, we will still do things that we don't want to. We will sit politely at dinner functions. We will dotingly sit through boring graduation ceremonies, Christmas concerts, and quietly stand in long lineups at the supermarket. Doing this does create a gentle kind of existence.

The key is that politeness should not allow others to hurt, manipulate, or take advantage of us. Politeness is not about being walked on, not having an opinion, or having to pretend to the point that we are numbed into oblivion. It is not about doing things we don't want to do while we slowly die inside.

It is simply about interacting in kindness.

And it's truly a lovely thing.

CHAPTER 5

SPENDING OUR ENERGY ON OTHERS

A few years ago, I found out that I was severely anemic. My hemoglobin was barely above life sustaining levels and I had no iron in my system. It took three blood transfusions to get me feeling human again. The doctors did all the tests to find out why I had been bleeding so heavily. They figured that I had been severely depleted for a long time. I had just returned from backpacking in Europe. For me to be travelling like that with such incredibly low levels meant that my system had been adjusting to extreme fatigue for a long time.

Beyond eating better, relaxing and taking iron supplements, I realized that some other big things were going to need to change in my life.

I had to fix all of the "energy leaks" in my system.

At this point, I was living downtown Toronto and newly single after being married for 20 years. On the relationship front, I was enjoying my newfound freedom immensely. Between dating apps, being a woman, and a population of 3,000,000 people, finding someone to have a drink with or fill my bed was easy.

But I also knew that it was draining me. And I really didn't have any energy within me to spare. So, after sowing a few wild oats, I decided to go completely celibate. Deep down, I knew that this was the first step.

After a few weeks, I started coming back into balance and I had the strangest sensation. I was standing in my living room and I had a feeling like my pelvic bowl had energetically tipped itself up in the front. More precisely, it had become level from front to back. I was suddenly aware that it had been tipping downwards in the front for as long as I could remember.

It was like any energy that came into my body would simply flow out of me.

I believe that in my teenage years, when I first started being interested in boys, some part of me decided that all of my energy would now flow towards them. It would flow towards anyone that I was interested in or who I wished would pay attention to me.

It was like being in a perpetual state of giving. No matter what came to me - no matter what I received - it would just flow right out of me into my husband, boyfriend or lover.

Of course, on a primal level, perhaps this makes sense. Once we come into the stage of life where finding a mate is of the utmost importance, we shift our energy patterns to find a partner. However, I would imagine that in nature, once this partner was found, we would then go back into our normal state of balance until we had babies and the energy would flow into them.

But now that my pelvis had energetically tilted upwards, the energy coming in was circulating within me instead. The circuit had closed. I was no longer perpetually leaking.

What was really interesting is that as soon as I felt this circuit close and the energy coming in was only nourishing *me*, I felt incredible guilt. How could I keep all of this for myself? There were so many people struggling. It was wrong for me to keep all of this just for me. I would be fine. I always had energy coming in. How could I not include others in what I was receiving?

Even as I was thinking this, I knew that it was not a healthy pattern. I was literally describing how I was being bled dry - energetically, emotionally and spiritually. This was a massive clue to just how leaky my system had been for a long time.

After this, I began recognizing many other leaks in my system. I started recognizing people in my life who were purely "takers" - the people who took advantage of my natural desire to give. Once I recognized them, I let them go. And if I couldn't distance myself from them due to them being family or at work, I just carefully observed our interactions. I practically watched the energy exchange and changed anything that I could.

Although I'm describing this in energetic terms, it isn't something psychic or supernatural. We can imagine that there is a coin jar that represents what is given and taken within an interaction. It was amazing to me how many people put absolutely nothing into the jar. In fact, many of these people only took from the jar. And the emptier the jar got, I would naively work harder to put more and more coins in.

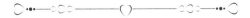

So Why Was I Doing It?

As much as I could point fingers at the others in my life whom I considered "takers", I also had to look at myself because I was playing a role too. What was inside of *me* that fit so perfectly with these people's personalities? We had to be matching puzzle pieces in some way. Their desire to take was perfectly matching my unending need to give. There were ideas and belief systems inside of me that were definitely playing a role here.

First of all, the idea of nourishing myself instead of others was truly a radical concept. It was like all the training I had ever received - either as a woman or a good Christian or a good member of society - was to be in a perpetual state of giving. To keep that energy for myself would be selfish. All must simply pass through.

But these ideas had also left me completely without energy for myself. I had been utterly exhausted for my whole adult life.

Fulfilling Unspoken Agreements

One place that I have spent a lot of energy is by holding myself to agreements with people that nobody ever agreed to out loud. I made assumptions and then filled in the blanks based on how I personally treated others.

For example, in my relationships with men, my tendency has been to always give more to the relationship than they do. I plan things. I try to get them to talk if they are upset. I try to keep the romantic fire going if they have become distant. There was some kind of unspoken agreement within me that this was my role.

With my in-laws, there was an unspoken agreement that I had to be a good daughter-in-law, that they were my elders, the grandparents of my children, and my husband's parents. That they were the leaders of the clan and I was not to cause trouble in the clan.

With my teachers at school and professors at university, they kind of held my future in their hands. My agreement was that I would give the answers required so that I would get the best marks. On occasion, there was a teacher who loved to be challenged. But for the most part, it was doing what I was told and being the model student that got me the grades to do what I wanted in life.

With my husband, we literally had a marital agreement with each other. But there was also an underlying agreement that I seemed to have signed that said that his feelings mattered more than mine. That it was my job to take care of him. That his career goals mattered more. That it was unfair for me to ask him to adapt or change. That raising the children shouldn't interrupt his busy day on the farm, etc etc.

He never asked me to do all of these things. This unwritten contract was all in my own mind and belief systems.

So, I started imagining sitting down and writing out these assumed contracts that I had with people. It was quite an eye-opener when I realized that if I had actually sat down with any of them with our contracts in front of us, there was no way I would have signed any of them!

It's like getting a new job. Let's say that the written agreement is that I need to work 40 hours per week, meet certain sales goals and find new clients. My boss's agreement is that he will pay me a certain amount each month. This is the basic, signed, "above the table" agreement.

But then, you walk into work on Monday morning and the boss is in a bad mood and he is taking it out on everyone. He is yelling and complaining that nothing is ever done right. The unwritten agreement is that as his employee, we must just listen and let him rant. We must smile and work even harder if he is in a bad mood.

Can you imagine if this had been part of the original agreement? Imagine that when you signed the paper, it said:

- You will receive $40,000 per year
- You will quietly listen to me yell and scream when I am in a bad mood
- You will sit in boring meetings and pretend that you're interested.
- If I am upset, you will work unpaid overtime in order to make me happy

Would you have signed this?

Or imagine you marry someone who likes to drink a lot and has a temper. Imagine the given agreement was:

- You will love me no matter how I treat you.
- You will clean up after me when I throw up because I was drinking
- You will put up with my insults and forgive me afterwards
- You will be the butt of my jokes and be fine with it
- I will contribute nothing to our romantic relationship

Would you have signed?

ABUSING OUR "MOTHER'S" INTUITION

(I put "Mother" in quotes because we all have this feminine intuition and it can be used against us whether we are a man, a woman, or have ever had children.)

A friend of mine shared a moment in her marriage where she suddenly became really angry. She realized that her husband had been using her empathy and intuition against her.

She realized that all he had to do was sigh loudly, take on a certain diminished posture or start to get upset and she would immediately drop what she was doing, change direction, and then try to fix whatever was bothering him.

What angered her the most is this was also how he would get his way if she was upset with him. She would have a genuine grievance and he would act like it was *her* attacking *him*. She would inevitably back off so that he was no longer "in pain".

But then she reflected on his childhood. He grew up in a family where showing emotion was not okay - for boys or girls. So, in order to be heard and seen, he learned to emote instead.

Emoting is how we silently send a message to mom. Because she is always "scanning the emotional airwaves", she will pick up on the fact that someone is unhappy. In this way, the children won't be criticized for feeling sad because they didn't complain. Mom just magically realized something and took us aside and asked us what's wrong. We didn't cry. We didn't ask for help. Mom just knew. We didn't have to say anything.

Well, my friend realized that this was exactly what was happening between her and her husband. When he was upset, he would just sulk, become obviously sad, quiet and withdrawn. He wouldn't say anything. He would just "go into his shell".

She would sense his sadness and then try to bring him out. The original grievance would be long forgotten and unfortunately nothing would be resolved.

USING OUR INTUITION IS PERFECTLY NATURAL

This is a natural part of being human – emotionally sensing those around us. It is designed to help us read children who cannot express themselves. It is great for helping adults who are traumatized in some way and can't express themselves. It is a natural human ability to help others. It's non-verbal communication. It's a very lovely, nurturing ability.

The problems begin when we start adjusting our lives based on what we are sensing from others.

In relationships, the partner who is more emotionally open will often be on full alert for the other. They know that their partner struggles to share their feelings. So, as soon as they become quiet, the first partner's need to connect will kick in, and their intuition would start to scan the airwaves trying to figure out what's going on with their partner.

And most people don't even know that they're doing it.

My friend's husband wasn't doing it consciously. He wasn't trying to control her. He had simply learned as a child that this was the only way to communicate disappointment or sadness. If he had spoken up or used his "feeling words" (unheard of 50 years ago), he would have been reprimanded because "boys don't cry" or he would be told that he was being too sensitive. This was simply a part of the culture at the time.

On the other hand, there are people who will use this to control others. When things don't go their way, they know that all they have to do is become quiet, ignore their partner and soon, the other will come around.

But again, my friend was also part of the problem. It was her who was constantly scanning the airwaves because she believed that she had to somehow fix the problems of another perfectly capable adult.

Taking the Room's Emotional Temperature

I have a wonderful friend, a 75-year-old Irish woman, who would always say to me, "Dear, we have to stop taking the emotional temperature of the room!"

Taking the "emotional temperature" is natural in a way. It's a primal self-preservation mechanism to let us know if danger is near. As we walk through the forest, we pay attention to what's around us. If something is close, we naturally try to "read" it to see if it is angry or irritated – a good clue that it could be dangerous and act erratically.

Similarly in life, we are taught to notice the emotions of those around us. If one of our parents had a bad temper, we would learn at a young age to stay away from them if they were in a bad mood. In couples, one person will often pay the most attention to the other's emotional state. Usually, it is the one who is calmest that will be highly attuned to the one that is most emotional or volatile – being a kind of emotional moderator for the other.

As a parent, we naturally read the emotions of our children. When they are small, they cannot explain to us what is going on. Our intuition must be able to tell us. Even as they grow, often they still cannot explain what is going on (especially in the teenage years). So, being able to get a sense of what's going on with them under the surface is not only helpful for them, it definitely helps the happiness of everyone in the house.

There's nothing wrong with this gift of having a sense of what's going on in the room unless we take it one step further and believe that we are somehow responsible for what happens there as well.

For example, maybe it is a family gathering and we know that *this sister* has an issue with *that uncle*. We know that there are hard feelings. We know that both are angry with each other and just being polite for the sake of the gathering.

And so, when we walk into the room, we naturally put out emotional feelers to each of the potential problems. We might keep the conversation light and away from topics that might cause them to blow. We might run interference between them keeping them apart. We might do all kinds of things to buffer any possible blowout.

But is this really our responsibility? Is it really up to us to make sure that others don't have issues or have conflict?

This is an incredible weight to bear. So, why do we do it?

BEING THE PEACE-KEEPER

Personally, I have always been the peace-keeper. It doesn't matter whether it was buffering my two sisters as children, sitting in meetings where people are fighting, being the buffer between my husband and his parents, or even gathering friends together and keeping the sparks from flying. There is something inside of me that has always felt that it was my role to keep everyone together and happy.

Although it is my nature, I also think that being the eldest of three children contributed too. This doesn't happen to all eldest children but in my family, it was easy to imagine how it happened.

My sister was born when I was 18 months old. You can imagine the scene. My new little sister is lying on a blanket on the floor with me at her side. My mom says, "Katrina, I'm just going to go to the bathroom. Please sit with your sister for a minute while I go." My mom takes ten steps to the bathroom and my little sister starts to cry. Mom says, "Katrina, what's wrong with Kristen? Put her soother in. Touch her. Talk to her. Just make her happy until I get there."

This is pretty powerful training to happen at 18 months old.

And of course, it continued. My youngest sister was born a couple years later. So, add together that I naturally like to care for people, I really wanted to help my mom, I never wanted to disappoint anyone, and the fact that it's really helpful to have an older sibling keep an eye on the younger ones, it is easy to see how this became embedded in my consciousness.

As the years went on, I was often still "in charge" of my sisters. There wasn't anything wrong with this. It was natural. I would want to go to the park with my friends. One or both of my sisters would want to come with me. My mom would say, "Katrina, please take your sisters with you. But make sure to watch them. You're responsible for them!" (As I write this, I am aware of how different it was in the 1970s when it was completely normal for young children to go to parks without their parents. Whereas this statement makes almost no sense today where parents accompany their children everywhere).

Now, let's say one of my sisters falls off the swing and gets hurt. I take her home and my parents easily might say, "Katrina, how could you let this happen?"

In no way am I blaming my parents for my people-pleasing ways. Growing up this way is a very natural training about how to care for others. This is how we learn to notice the people around us. How to help them. It's a wonderful training.

Plus, I am a mother. I fully understand where my parents were coming from. It's natural to ask children to look out for each other. We can't have eyes everywhere. This observation isn't about blame. It's simply identifying the places where this deep training of being hyper-aware of how others are feeling comes from.

And of course, there are times that we *should* help out. We can bring insight into a family argument to try to heal a relationship. We can mediate and find solutions in meetings. And we can definitely do what we can to find peaceful resolutions between friends and family.

However, there is that point where we step over a line from simply contributing as part of the group to feeling responsible for the outcome. There is something inside people-pleasers that cannot rest if there is any conflict between others and we will go to great lengths to make everything okay all of the time.

But this is not our responsibility and the outcome often has nothing to do with us.

I recently had an interesting experience. While sitting with two old friends, a heated argument began. Now, both of these friends are big personalities with strong opinions. If things get heated, neither one is likely to back down. For the last 25 years, I would have jumped in and tried to cushion the argument. I would have tried to be the "human whisperer" saying things like "I think what she really means is this" and "I think the reason that you're so angry about what she said is this". Somehow, I've always felt that I needed to stop whatever was going to happen.

Well, as this particularly heated topic was raised, these guys were on opposite sides. For a little while, I interjected my thoughts and contributed where I could. But then one friend started screaming at the other and the other didn't back down.

Maybe it was the experiences that I share in this book. Maybe it was my choice to do things out of love for me. Either way, I quietly left the porch and went for a walk. I left them to their fury and trusted that whatever happened happened.

When I returned, one had left and gone home. Strangely enough, I wasn't affected one way or the other. I love both of them. I would have loved to have spent more time as the three of us. But what happened between them was very real. Both had issues brewing inside of them about the other and so maybe they really needed to have this blowout.

Walking away from this was an absolutely brand-new experience for me. Never in my 49 years had I been able to walk away from two people arguing. I had always tried to make it better.

And yet, this felt so peaceful. I let them be themselves. I let myself be me. No angst. No worry. No energy spent.

I really liked it better this way.

CHAPTER 6

LIVING IN OTHER PEOPLE'S REALITIES

At one point in my travels, I stayed with a friend who had married a Greek man who was very "passionate". My friend was British, romantic and loved life. After falling in love with this man, she quickly had to adjust to his way of speaking to her. If he yelled at her and she was hurt by it, he would just say that she didn't understand the Greek culture. That he didn't mean it the way she thought. That she just had to adjust to people raising their voices and yelling. It was normal - just a different way of communicating.

So... she did. She adjusted and adjusted and adjusted to the point that, 20 years later, she was barely the romantic woman that she had once been. There was some of her old self because she would always remind me to look at the beautiful moon and smell all of the different flowers. But the reality was that this very gentle spirit had had to develop a necessary harsh exterior.

I related to this a lot.

I was 23 years old when I fell in love and married the brother of my friend from University. He was gorgeous, funny and of all things, a farmer. Well, I had grown up in Toronto - a true city girl. Farms were something that we looked at in picture books or saw in a movie once in a while. I knew that they existed but I definitely had no idea what it would be like to live on one.

I had begun visiting the farm just as a friend. So the fact that I didn't fit in was kind of interesting, cute and quirky. I was just that crazy city girl who studied mathematics and didn't know anything about farming. But there was actually much more that I didn't understand.

While sitting around the kitchen table with his family and friends, I really struggled to relate to how they saw the world. They were "country-folk", fundamentalist Christians, and Dutch. Now, there isn't anything wrong with any of these demographics (and they certainly had many lovely qualities), but I just couldn't understand many of their opinions.

Why were all other religions going to hell? Why were gay people not allowed to be ministers? Why was getting pregnant out of wedlock such a sin? Why couldn't men change their own baby's diapers? Why did the farm rule and women just served their husbands and the farm?

It was all so beyond me.

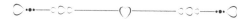

ADAPTING TO THE FARM

Of course, visiting a place is very different than living there. When I was just visiting as a friend from University, I could observe these people as interesting specimens from a culture that I simply knew nothing about. There was a comfortable distance in that. However, falling in love with my friend's brother and realizing that I would likely spend the rest of my life there was a whole different story.

Although I was educated, well-loved by my family, forward-thinking and curious about philosophy, life and anything in particular, my greatest desire was to be loved and to have a happy marriage. I wanted this to work. I wanted to have the fairy-tale life where we all got along. Where his parents loved me. Where he and I happily milked the cows with smiling children at our sides, his family and friends all around - a picture-perfect, happy, rural experience.

But I was struggling to figure out how to fit in. How I saw the world was just so different than the world I was blending into.

WHEN IN ROME

I still remember the moment that I gave up a part of who I was.

I was trying to sort out how I could fit in peacefully and be really happy. It felt like I was playing with an inner Rubik's cube, trying to see how I could contort and change myself to make this work. However, I eventually realized that there were parts of me that would never fit in. They just couldn't.

Plus, I was only 23 years old. I really didn't know who I was. I had no idea what parts of me were important and which ones weren't. And I was so in love. This was all I ever wanted.

So, torn between marrying the man I loved and maintaining unknown parts of me that might get lost in the shuffle, I remember the day when my new mantra appeared in my life "Well, Katrina, when in Rome, do as the Romans".

And that was that. A corner had been turned. A promise made. I would keep what I could of who I was. But I would give up what I had to in order to fit into this strange land.

In that moment, I decided to blend in. I figured that if I brought all of my city ideas to the farm, it just wouldn't work. If I brought my ideas about spirituality and religion, I would be constantly arguing with everyone. We would never be at peace.

I decided that if I was going to thrive there, I had to learn from them. I had to mimic them. I had to learn about what worked in this world.

So, I did what the other farm-wives did. I made lunches for the men-folk. I milked the cows. I tried to keep my husband happy. I went to dinner at my in-laws every Sunday and tried to not cause too much trouble with my different opinions. (Mind you, I am sure that my in-laws would say that I was absolutely opinionated. But there was just so much more within me that I buried that simply could never come out.)

And in some ways, and in some circumstances, "learning the ropes" by copying others is a good idea.

Unless you totally lose yourself as I certainly did.

LEAVING ROME

My great crisis came six years after I got married in 1999. I had lumps growing in my breast and all of the lies I had been telling myself about my life and how happy I was came crashing down around me. My mom had died four years earlier of cancer and now I had found lumps growing in my breast like she had. I didn't want to die like my mom and her mom had. I really wanted to live.

Luckily, a man named Jim (the teacher I mention in Chapter 3) appeared in our lives who had incredible healing gifts. Back in 1987, he had been electrocuted when the extension ladder he was carrying hit an overhead electrical wire. Whether he died and came back or just nearly died is unknown. But, when he "returned to the world", he was psychic, empathic, and incredibly wise. And through prayer, he had abilities to heal others - if that was their path.

I was so thankful that he would work with me to help me heal and to understand why all the women in my family were dying of cancer. Through this process, he became my first true spiritual teacher - opening me up to the world that deep down I knew about but had never had the opportunity to put into words or see in a real human being.

At this point in my life, the greatest blessing of this man was that he could see me for who I really was. He saw beyond the frustrated farm-wife, the exhausted mom, and all of the stories that I had been telling myself. As he asked me questions, I began realizing how much of myself I had buried in order to fit in. I realized how many of my own thoughts I had questioned because it went against his family, friends and the community surrounding us.

I also realized that trying to fit in like this was slowly killing me. I was actually quite depressed because I truly didn't see a way out or any chance that anything was ever going to change.

There is a story about a frog that sits in a pot of room-temperature water. If the heat is increased slowly enough, the frog will simply adjust to the water temperature and not jump out. Eventually, the water reaches the boiling point and the frog simply dies. The frog never thought of jumping out because it never noticed that the water getting warmer. However, if you were to heat the pot to boiling and throw the frog in, it would instantly jump out to save itself.

This is what can happen when we live according to other people's beliefs.

It can happen in families. But it is even more apparent in couples. We want a loving connection with them so badly that we will slowly adjust ourselves, and even our world-view, to adapt to their way of seeing things. Our truth still lives within us. But instead of us standing tall in our beliefs and potentially causing any conflict or tension, we will just let those parts of our truth and who we are quietly slip away.

CHAPTER 7

STOP REACHING SO FAR...
OR REACHING AT ALL

Back on the island... My hosts were home unexpectedly one day because it was a bank holiday. The house was open-concept and they liked to watch TV really, really loud which meant that you really couldn't do anything else except hear the TV. I soon realized that there was no way I was going to get any work done on this day.

What was worse was that it was pouring rain outside. I wouldn't even be able to escape for a walk to get away from the constant noise. I was trapped inside for the day. *Sigh*.

This wouldn't have been so bad if it wasn't for the huge disconnect that I felt with them. I had been there for four weeks now and I still never knew whether they were happy with me or mad at me. They were polite enough but mostly they just ignored me - like a tenant living in the back corner. Honestly, sometimes I felt like one of their belongings - like they would tell their friends, "Yes, this is our house. This is our son. This is our Canadian. This is our kitchen."

It was like I wasn't even a person. And honestly, it was wearing me down. But maybe today would be better. Maybe today my hostess would want to do something together where I could help her with her English. That was why I was here, yet we hadn't done anything beyond polite niceties for weeks. Hopefully today would be different.

I walked out into the living room where they were all sitting on the couch in front of the TV. They were partly watching the Walking Dead and partly just playing on their phones and iPads.

I leaned over the back of the couch and said to my hostess, "Hey, if you want to hang out and play Scrabble or something, I'm here."

She replied, "Yes, I am busy right now. But we will see."

I returned to my room. All I could hear was The Walking Dead screeching in French. My emotions were getting pretty raw and truthfully I was getting quite lonely and down. God I wanted to get out of there.

The rain had started to slow down. Maybe I could go for a walk. That would be cleansing and peaceful. Yes. I'll go for a walk to the beach. It was about a 25 minute walk. It will be perfect.

I walked out into the living room and said, "I'm going for a walk." But there was no reaction from the couch. *Sigh.*

As I walked away from the house, the sound of the Walking Dead began to disappear. The coolness of the rain on my hair, running down my face, started to soothe my confusion.

As I walked by the banana fields, with the rain running down my face, I began to cry. I felt so alone - like I didn't exist. No matter what I did, nothing helped. I couldn't reach them.

Was something wrong? What's going on? Why am I still here? Why don't I leave?

As I felt this horrible emptiness starting to take over, I began imagining people who were raised in homes like this - and worse. Was this what it felt like to be raised in a home where you were simply another mouth to feed without any real connection? No real awareness or compassion for your thoughts and feelings?

How did people survive this and turn out to be any kind of normal? Would they ever be able to have a loving relationship?

I was 49 years old. I was raised in a very loving home. I had people all over the world who truly loved me. Yet, four weeks in a disconnected, yet polite, home was making me absolutely crazy. I began having doubts about myself. I began thinking that I was simply a loser - that I was completely lost in life.

And of course, none of these thoughts were true. Yet, it was like the emptiness and depression were just creating these ideas to fill the void. And because I was lacking the connection and any reflection of those around me, I was believing them.

Was I supposed to be experiencing this for some reason? To have compassion for those who were raised like this? To understand what it must be like to have had this during your formative years?

After a while, I arrived at the beach. I was dripping wet. My shoes were soaked. But I was starting to feel happier, lighter in some way.

I found a picnic table and just sat in the rain looking at the ocean. I took a few deep breaths and tears started flowing down my face. Nothing big. Just a release. Perhaps letting the pressures of my travels go. Maybe just forgiving myself for taking everything so personally.

Or maybe I was just thankful for being alone out in the rain by this magnificent ocean. I don't know.

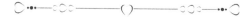

LIVING WITHOUT CONNECTION

Let's imagine that we define love as the connection between us. How much we feel loved by someone can be described as how deeply we feel the connection[1].

Not feeling this connection is hard for everyone but it is especially hard for people-pleasers because we value connecting above all. This could be with total strangers at a café, our friends, children or partners. We just love that feeling of being connected to another person.

I think that many people-pleasers are actually very empathic - that we easily feel the emotions of others. Because we can feel what others are feeling, we are able to help them more. So, if others are shut down, we kick our people-pleasing connectors into an even higher gear. Every moment is spent unconsciously or consciously trying to figure out how to reach them.

BUILDING BRIDGES

For me, it feels like building bridges - like I'm perpetually building bridges towards other people.

Imagine a people-pleaser married to someone who is emotionally unavailable. What will they spend their life doing? Building emotional bridges to their partner. Why? Because they want to feel connected. They want to love. They want to truly communicate. They want to experience true union with the one that they love.

---

[1] This topic is explored deeply in my book *Tantric Intimacy*.

But if the other person isn't wired that way, then unfortunately, it just doesn't matter how many bridges you build, they are not going to embrace you as you walk across. It's like they are content on their side of the river and after all of your hard work building the bridge across to them, you blissfully walk across it hoping to fall into their arms. But instead they just turn, look at you and say "Hey" and they go back to whatever they were doing.

In the host family I lived with, I felt this so acutely. In many ways, they provided me such a wonderful opportunity. But there was just no emotional connection. There was no intimacy.

But *my* soul just isn't wired that way. I must connect. And there is something in me - maybe an eternal optimist - who will keep on trying. I will try every way I can think of. Maybe through conversation, doing things for them, humour, doing things together, anything. But, in this situation, although they were polite to me, most of the time it was like talking into an empty chamber.

STILL BEING A GIVER

I found myself wanting to retreat. I wanted to judge these people for how I felt they were treating me. But I knew that they weren't doing anything on purpose. I was just hurting. So, maybe I wanted to withdraw so that I would feel like the one choosing to pull away instead of being the one left out and ignored.

But this isn't just wasn't my nature.

Ralph Waldo Emerson once said, "The love you withhold is the pain you carry."

I didn't want to stop being loving. There is great joy in giving. There is great joy in being a nice person. There is nothing wrong with this.

I love looking for the good in people. I don't like to focus on what is wrong with someone. I want to find a happy connection no matter how quirky each of us might be.

So, I decided to still love and continue to give simply because that was who I was and it brought me joy. It wasn't to make them happy or to make them like me. I would just do it because that's who I am. No questions asked.

It reminded me of a poem that they found on the wall of Mother Teresa's room by Dr. Kent called *The Paradoxical Commandments*:

People are often unreasonable, illogical and self centred;
Forgive them anyway.
If you are kind, people may accuse you of selfish, ulterior motives;
Be kind anyway.
If you are successful, you will win some false
friends and some true enemies;
Succeed anyway.
If you are honest and frank, people may cheat you;
Be honest and frank anyway.
What you spend years building, someone could destroy overnight;
Build anyway.
If you find serenity and happiness, they may be jealous;
Be happy anyway.
The good you do today, people will often forget tomorrow;
Do good anyway.
Give the world the best you have, and it may never be enough;
Give the world the best you've got anyway.
You see, in the final analysis, it is between you and your God;
It was never between you and them anyway.

I love this poem.

THE TURNING POINT

CHAPTER 8

WHO YOU ARE IS IMPORTANT

At another point in my travels, I decided to visit Malta, a tiny island in the Mediterranean. After travelling around Ireland and Scotland in January, I thought a little warmth and sunshine would be just the thing.

I had chosen a little place through AirBnB, as opposed to heading to one of the resorts, and I assumed that it would be a little spot in a decent-sized city. But as the taxi cab wound its way to the tiny town on the south shore where my place was, I was really starting to wonder where he was taking me.

All of the buildings seemed destroyed. There were crumbling homes and apartments everywhere. Nothing seemed to be cared for. There were people walking along the highway that definitely looked like they'd had a tough go in life. As the taxi drove into the little town, I was getting concerned. The homes just looked like lined-up cement structures and I couldn't tell if they were inhabited, deserted or if it was just a very poor neighbourhood.

When I got to my place, it was actually lovely inside - like *really* lovely. My hostess was absolutely wonderful, friendly and so hospitable. She was Maltese and she loved her country. She was passionate about sharing the culture and her island. She was truly wonderful.

The next day, I went for a walk. Most people I saw were British expats (Britain had owned Malta up until 1964). But once in a while, I would see an authentic Maltese person. As I passed them, I would try to smile at them. But they just bowed their heads and walked away quickly so as not to make eye contact. When I went to the small restaurants in the village, I was initially treated the same way.

Honestly, I felt like quite an intruder. That was the only vibe I got - suspicion and the idea that I shouldn't be there. That I should leave them alone.

So, this would cause me to be even friendlier than normal. I'm naturally pretty friendly. But there is another gear that we can go into when we really want to put someone at ease. When they found out that I was from Canada, that often helped. I would ask them questions about Malta, talk about my children and about being a farmer. And by the time the meal was served, they would have taken me under their wing like I was a local.

A few days later, my fellow tenant and I decided to take a bus-ride into Valletta, the capital city. In many ways, Valletta is very beautiful - beautiful architecture, the sea, statues, churches, etc. (and I got to eat pastizzi from a street vendor - a classic Maltese food that my family friend used to feed us when we were children).

But truthfully, I found it very strange walking around. The architecture was a collection of all the cultures that had ruled Malta over the centuries (and millennia). There were signs of all the wealth of the conquering nations like Britain, France, the Arab nations, Sicily, etc.

But where was Malta? Where was the soul of the original people?

JUST LIKE US

Suddenly Malta felt like me.

How long had I been governed by others? How often had I internalized the beliefs of my parents, family, or friends? In school, I had done exactly what my teacher wanted me to do in order to get good grades? I had listened to what society thought about the role of women, doing what we're told, and being a "good person"?

And I know that I am by far not the worst off. There are so many people who have been abused by their parents, priests, or partners. From the time they were born, they were taken over completely - forced to do as they're told - with the threat of violence, ridicule or abandonment hanging over their heads.

In many ways, I feel like our psyches are a lot like the city of Valletta. There are all of these huge constructs that might look great from the outside but they were built by others. We were just the real-estate that housed their pride, ideals, and conquests.

And to make matters worse, this real-estate is also the field for many battles and torment - none of which had anything to do with us. This could look like parents working out their personal sadness and abuse by hurting their children. It could be children being used as pawns in a bitter divorce. It could be the church-goer wracked with guilt because they had an impure thought.

But none of this has anything to do with the person themselves. It is all about other people. It is only *other people's* drama simply playing out within us.

As an example, during the second world war, Malta was ruled by Britain. Because of its strategic position, it was used as an aircraft base and was therefore attacked mercilessly - to the point that Churchill called it "Britain's Unsinkable Aircraft Carrier".

Malta suffered incredible destruction in battles that had nothing to do with her.

Does this sound familiar?

WHAT HAPPENS WHEN WE ARE FREE?

So now, let's imagine what happens to the Maltese people when the British give them their sovereignty back? Malta had been ruled by others for as long as anyone could remember.

Who is left when we finally get rid of the conquerors?

This can also happen in our own healing journey. We heal and integrate what happened to us in our childhood. We change our personal patterns to stop attracting abusive partners. We increase our own self-worth and start standing up for ourselves.

But then sometimes we find ourselves in a very lonely place. Not only are we lonely because we don't relate to many of the people in our lives, we actually don't really know who *we* are anymore.

I have a good friend who is part of the Alcoholics Anonymous program. She had a horrible upbringing filled with violence, neglect and substance abuse that no child (or person) should ever have to endure. Since joining AA, and doing an incredible amount of personal work, she has come a long way and has become an incredibly wise woman with a lot to share with the world.

One day, she was heading to a retreat and we were talking about a certain drama that was playing out in her life. It was reminiscent of all the controlling people she had grown up with and she was struggling to separate herself from the pain and drama that was rising within her.

As we chatted about this, I suddenly asked her, "So, who were you before the world started throwing punches at you?"

She looked at me, tears rose in her eyes and she said, "I have no fucking idea."

The problem is that what we experience as children is our first experience being alive. As a baby, we form what we understand about the world. We are learning about people. We learn what is right and wrong based on what our parents praise or reprimand us for.

We also learn what the goals of life are. Maybe it is to get married, buy a house, have two children and have an upstanding job. Maybe it's to live close to the earth, living off the land, and being one with nature. Maybe it's thriving in corporate America. Or maybe it's simply about surviving and living on welfare.

Within that specific perspective, we also develop our own personality. We may learn to be defensive as self-protection. We may become a rebel because we deeply disapprove of what our parents or the society we grew up in believes and preaches. We may believe that people always want something from us because we were either abused or people only gave us things when there were strings attached.

Within these experiences, we mix in our own true nature. We become a complex weaving of our actual nature and our upbringing. So, it's often hard to sort them out.

So we can imagine that at some point when we realize that we have been "eating eyeballs" to make others happy, to be loved, or to fit in, it can be quite a challenging journey to figure out why we are doing it, where these ideas came from, and how to move past it.

BECOMING SOVEREIGN

I love the phrase "becoming sovereign" because it basically means that now *we* get to be the king or queen of our own land. *We* get to make the rules. *We* get to decide who we let into our country. *We* get to be the judge of whether something is right or wrong for us.

There is no longer another governing body that is able to judge us — not our spouse, the church, our parents, community, family, anyone. We get to be on top of our own mountain.

But even once we are free and allowed to make our own choices, we may feel completely lost. We see this in parents whose children move out. Their lives have been so completely defined by taking care of and making their children happy, 20 years later, they are empty inside. They have forgotten who they were before they had babies.

Sometimes, when we aren't used to being allowed to have our own identity, we may find someone or something else to define our lives for us again. We may marry again, join a group that has a strong philosophy of living, or simply start worrying about what strangers think or the neighbours. It's like we just don't know how to be sovereign.

And like Malta, it may have been many generations since anyone was king or queen of their own land. If Malta had had just had one conquering nation take over for 50 years, there would still be people who knew the Maltese culture intrinsically. But when you've been run by others for thousands of years, there are few people left to tell us who we genuinely are.

Similarly, if we come from generations of people-pleasers, then it might be difficult to find anyone in our family to look to as role models. So instead, we must dig deep within ourselves and define who we are - perhaps for the first time in generations.

Chapter 9

Being My Big Beautiful Self

One night, back on the island, my hostess took me out with her friends to play bingo.

At this time, I was still wrestling with the weird laundry/dishes issue. I hadn't eaten the eyeballs and I was struggling with eating many of the traditional dishes that she had prepared for me. We had gone out many times with her friends by now - each time leaving me this mute child in the corner not understanding the language, sometimes for days at a time. I was struggling with my inability to read my hostess. I just couldn't feel a connection. I was coming up blank all of the time.

As I sat there putting beans on my Bingo cards (which I really enjoyed because I could actually understand the French and I was feeling very bilingual), I was thinking about why all of these seemingly small issues were bothering me so much. Why wasn't I able to just be me? Why couldn't I share who I was instead of just drowning trying to fit into their world?

Then I saw a man walk by with a huge diamond-studded Playboy-bunny earring. And suddenly, Hugh Hefner, the creator of Playboy, came into my mind. I had never really thought of him before.

Interesting thoughts began running through my mind. *I'll bet he never cared what anyone ever thought of him. I'll bet he just did whatever he wanted. He wanted to fill a mansion with Playboy bunnies and walk around in a robe smoking a pipe. He wanted to create a nudie magazine. So he did it. He didn't care at all what anyone else thought.*

This was revolutionary to me... and annoying. Hadn't I already figured this out? Hadn't I already released being so attached to what other people thought?

This had been a big part of my personal journey from my first book, *What If You Could Skip the Cancer?*. I had begun to stop taking all of my orders from everyone around me and shift instead to God, myself, and the personal intuitive connection there. That was 20 years ago! Hadn't I already figured this out?

Well, within my confusion, at this bingo game, Mr. Hefner represented something important for me – an icon (although perhaps an extreme one surrounded by controversy). Regardless, it was the strength of him standing in his character that was blowing my hair back. Doing what he wanted regardless of what other people thought.

In this moment, *this* was the medicine I needed. And I started to feel a little inner strength returning.

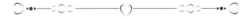

BEING ALLOWED TO BE UNIQUE

There is something magical about getting to be yourself without apology. Or even simply knowing that you don't need to explain yourself.

I once had a friend who has high-functioning autism. You wouldn't have known it from the outside. He just looked like a quiet, shy guy. But once you got to know him you would start noticing interesting things about him.

For example, he couldn't lie. This included weird pleasantries, being falsely polite, and doing things that he didn't want to do. He was also only able to live in the present moment. Because of this, it was hard for him to plan for future events, or have abstract thoughts like excitement or worry about anything.

But it wasn't always easy because as a society, we often tell white lies. So he tended to withdraw from most social situations because he couldn't relate to why people were saying what they were saying and acting outside of their truth.

Being his friend really helped me to look at the world through different glasses. I saw how often we did things that we didn't want to do but we just did them out of obligation (he couldn't understand this at all). I learned how to live in the present moment so much more - not focusing on the future or wishing I could redo the past.

But most of all, he allowed a new freedom within me to be as quirky and unique as I truly was. I didn't have to hide or swallow anything. I could just be me.

For example, I have always felt - especially as a teacher and writer - that I needed to be digestible to the masses. I never wanted to insult anyone. I never wanted to upset any particular interest group or demographic.

So, this often meant that I would water down important concepts to the point that the real message was completely lost. And so, anyone who was looking for them and ready for them didn't get the goods. It was like the rules of politeness had extended into my writing and business and had hand-cuffed me for fear of upsetting anyone.

One day, while discussing being on the autism spectrum, he said to me, "But doesn't everyone think differently?"

And of course, the answer is "yes".

Imagine if each of us were allowed to think however we wanted. What if there was no "normal"? What if there were simply 7 billion different ways that brains worked? How empowering would that be?

After all, who decided what was typical and atypical? Or normal and abnormal? Certainly it was based on the minds of those people who decided.

DUMBING DOWN

When I was young, I was very good in school.

Because school is such a huge part of our lives when we are young, and the education system uses our academic achievements to rank us, I was always very sensitive that my getting good grades might make others feel badly. I had no need to be above or ahead of anyone. I really didn't want to be a part of this sorting system.

This is one of my criticisms with the education system. It only praises those who learn and can be tested in the identical ways as the people who created the system. It's like only the squirrels get A's when squirrels make the school. And the fish feel crappy about themselves because they aren't good at climbing trees.

My worst moment of high school was in 9th grade history class. At this point, I still really loved school. I loved learning and I hadn't figured out that this wasn't cool yet (in the 1980s being smart was only for nerds and geeks).

We had a particularly horrible teacher. He didn't teach anything. He was boring. He berated the students and was really just a jerk and the class treated him as such.

Well, one day, we had a test. I knew that we weren't learning anything in class, so I just studied the textbook. I diligently studied everything I could because at this point, doing well was important to me.

Well, the test came and it was absolutely unfair. He didn't test anything that had been talked about in class. Everything was from the textbook - and mostly hidden in the footnotes.

The next day, he walked into the room with the stack of tests and glared at the room. He told everyone that they were a bunch of losers. He said that they would never amount to anything. He said that he had never met such a bunch of lazy, pathetic, stupid kids.

One brave student said, "You can't blame us for getting a bad mark on your test. It was totally unfair. You are a horrible teacher. It isn't us."

At this point, the most evil smile came onto his face and he said, "OH YA?! Guess what, it isn't me at all. Every single one of you failed miserably except one person. Katrina got 100%. Now who's the bad teacher?"

You have to understand that even today, I'm still a little shy. But back then as a 13-year-old quiet girl, I literally wanted to die. There was just nowhere to go.

At that moment, I decided that I would never be singled out again to make anyone else feel badly about themselves.

For the next couple years, I made sure I never got 100% again by putting wrong answers on tests. I downplayed my intelligence as much as I could. I hung out with the drug and party crowd. I even got arrested and ended up in jail shortly after this incident by getting drunk at a pre-teen dance.

I tried anything to shake this horrible feeling that who I was and how my brain worked was going to isolate me for the rest of my life.

OUT IN THE WORLD

This dumbing down continued for decades. I had no interest in preaching to people about things or correcting them or anything like that. If people were talking about something that wasn't accurate, sometimes I would speak up. But most of the time I would just let them keep talking - especially if they were men.

If they were women, it was somehow easier to just offer a different opinion and we would have a conversation, a debate or a laugh. But many of the men around me would become defensive, arrogant or just become painfully quiet. They said that I thought I was better than them, that I was trying to make them look bad, that I thought I was "sooo smart".

It didn't take long for me to just let them think whatever they wanted and get on with my life. It didn't matter anyway.

However, it actually *did* matter.

Why shouldn't I contribute equally to a conversation? Why did my opinion not count? Why couldn't the men handle being contradicted if what they were saying was incorrect?

This is a dynamic that isn't as prevalent now as it was in previous generations. But it still whispers... Let the man think he's smart. Let him think he knows. It will make him feel masculine... and then maybe if he steps into his masculine, then we will have the chance to feel feminine.

It is definitely an old way of thinking. But it still exists. So it's good to be aware.

CHAPTER 10

THE ABILITY TO BE ALONE

One of the biggest reasons that I have eaten so many eyeballs in my life is because honestly, I have been afraid to be alone. Being alone meant that no one liked me. That I wasn't like everyone else. Like I was unchosen, unattractive and that no one wanted to be with me.

This is certainly why I didn't speak up enough in my marriage. I was so thrilled that this man that I loved so much loved me back, I would have done anything to make him happy.

In fact, for the first few years, I would wake up every morning hoping that he hadn't changed his mind about marrying me. Maybe it was feeling like a geeky outsider in high school that made me believe that I wasn't loveable. But the bottom line was that this awesome guy loved me and I wasn't going to screw it up.

And so, if something happened and I was upset about it, I would easily swallow it. I wanted to be the most supportive, strong, amazing wife ever. This guy was never going to wake up and wonder why he married me.

This, coupled with the fact that I truly believed in being married forever and my pride couldn't have handled getting divorced, meant that there were a lot of reasons for me to just stay quiet, do the "right" thing and keep the peace.

Being Happy Alone

Because of some of the stories I've told, it might sound like my marriage was terrible. But it wasn't. We had many wonderful times. We supported each other through illness, death, children, running businesses and a million other things. But we were also very human and very young when we were married and being married isn't always easy. So, after 20 years, we amicably divorced and went our separate ways.

After a few years of dating many different men, going celibate, and having all kinds of "aha moments", I finally came to a place of wholeness. But first, I had to come to peace with being alone. I had to create a life that I loved whether I had a significant other in my life or not.

I needed to get to the place where I truly loved my own company.

My Spinster Turning Point

There were so many times in those years when I felt so lonely. Why was I alone? Had I taken a wrong turn? Had I done something wrong?

One night I was at a friend's house and was sharing with him and his wife how I was really struggling with this loneliness. His wife suddenly got this excited look on her face and passed me the book *Spinster* by

Kate Bolick. Deep down, I was furious. How insensitive! How could she do that? Was she calling me a dried-up spinster? Who did she think she was?

But I took it home because I'm just like that and it sat on a shelf in the corner of my apartment for the next few months. It just sat there staring at me reminding me just how alone and what a loser I was.

Deep down, I didn't really believe this. I knew I was on a journey somewhere. I was okay. But the thought of this book held all the fears that we easily can be susceptible to when we are faced with being alone - feeling unloved, unwanted and unchosen.

Then one New Year's Day, I woke up completely depressed. It was one of those days where I didn't think I could feel any worse. As my eyes gazed around my apartment, that wretched book lit up like a Christmas tree.

I guess the time had come to bite the bullet and read the damn book.

Well, to my surprise, it was an absolute turning point for me.

The original spinsters weren't ugly, dried-up women that no one wanted. They were women who were able to work, make money and be independent when it just wasn't an option for women anywhere.

Historically, women weren't allowed to work - even just 100 years ago here in North America. But they *were* allowed to work in textile mills. And although they were paid less than men, these women actually had their own money. Plus, they would also have a room or flat in a boarding house just for spinsters.

They were independent women with their own money and own place to live. In a time when a woman's identity was completely dependent on finding a good husband, these spinsters were superheroes. They didn't have to get married to be a person. They could pay their own rent. They could choose their own entertainment. They could choose to do anything they wanted.

This was incredibly radical for the time!

Many of these women had chosen to not get married after watching their friends and sisters instantly become servants of their husbands. This wasn't evil. It was the norm.

Even within my lifetime, our home economics textbooks had lessons in "How to be a good wife". They included how to keep your husband happy, how to support him in his work, how to keep the children quiet because he's had a bad day, and my favourite, don't forget to clean up a little and put a ribbon in your hair - let him know that you care enough to not share your difficulties of the day with him.

This was normal. And in no way do I think those rules were written by men. This isn't oppression. These school curriculums were written by other women who had learned efficient ways of keeping men happy. Of being the best servant you could be. And do you know why? Because if for some reason, that marriage didn't work out and you either got a divorce or were kicked out in the street, you were done. Whatever you loved about your life would no longer exist.

So, these excellent rules of servitude were actually a kindness they were bestowing onto the next generation. How to be the happiest, most loving servant. And how to do it with a smile.

So, you can imagine the decision these spinsters had to make. Do they give up their wonderful independence, economic, intellectual, and personal?

Well, I'm sure some did. But a lot didn't.

So, what do you think the men of that time would have thought of these independent women? Would they have looked at them with respect and intrigue? Probably not. These women would have been classified as headstrong, difficult, impossible to control, and unattractive. It might have been decided that they were obviously undesirable and unintelligent since they did not choose a life of marriage to one of them.

It's easy to imagine how the idea of being a spinster would be passed down through the generations as being a horrible fate that obviously meant that there was something wrong with YOU.

Well, this gave my life a completely different spin. Here I was in my own apartment, self-sufficient, healthy, strong, and well-loved complaining about the very freedoms that these women fought so hard to achieve.

I had arrived. Was I really lonely? No, not really. I was happy, peaceful and pretty great actually. There were just these strange thoughts running through my head that told me that I had to be lonely. Why was no one here? Why was I alone in bed? Was there something wrong with me? Am I too ugly? Too fat? Too difficult? Too much?

Of course, none of these were true. These were just remnants of this very strange tradition of assuming that if someone chooses to be an individual instead of being part of a couple that there must be something wrong. But it's just not true.

HAPPY AND TRULY WHOLE

From here I grew differently. I became who I actually was. I realized that I was wonderfully happy in my own company. I had lots of friends to have adventures with. And that I loved having adventures on my own.

It brought me into a wonderful place of choice. Suddenly if I didn't like something that was going on in a relationship, I didn't have to swallow it and accept it because I was trying to fit into someone else's world. I now assumed that being 100% honest all the time is the answer. And if that means that we have to go our separate ways, that's perfect.

It's a radical thing when we don't *need* to have a partner. If we love our own company and the company of friends, then we won't choose to be with someone who makes us sad, angers us, embarrasses us, talks down to us, bores us, or that generally just doesn't make our moments better or more interesting.

We won't eat any eyeballs just to keep someone else happy.

I remember the first couple of dates with one particularly lovely man. We were chatting about this idea of being whole whether we had a partner or not. And I shared with him that I was actually completely happy and content in my life right now. I didn't need someone in my life. But if he wanted to play the masculine to my feminine (I'm really into the dance of polarities in relationship[2]), then I would love to spend time with him.

He looked at me and said, "So you don't need me for anything?"

"Nope."

"Then why do you want to be with me?"

"Because I *choose* to be with you. I don't *need* to be with you. This is very different."

He thought about it a bit and then smiled. And a wonderful relationship ensued.

---

[2]   I discuss this further in my book, *Tantric Intimacy*

CHAPTER 11

BEING TRULY HONEST WITH OURSELVES

Back on the island, it was actually a young woman of 18 who broke me open and helped me to start being truly honest with myself. We were all out with the group and she and I ended up chatting alone.

In broken English, she asked me, "Why did you choose to come to this island?"

I said, "Well, I didn't choose it. My hostess chose *me*. I didn't know anything about it."

She said, "It must be so hard for you - not understanding anything all of the time. We don't even speak a kind of French that you would recognize from Canada. It is a kind of "ghetto-French" and it's so mixed with Creole, you wouldn't have a chance at understanding."

At this, tears started to rise inside of me. But I didn't want to cry. I didn't want to cry in front of everyone and make things weird. I knew that they wouldn't understand. I would just feel stupid and exposed. This was no place to cry.

But something had been leaked. My seal had been broken. There was no going back now. I soon realized that I wanted to go home. I was finished here. I had no heart left for it.

I didn't want to disappoint my hostess. But I needed to go home.

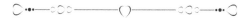

WHAT REALITY ARE YOU TRYING TO CONVINCE YOURSELF OF?

When I first watched the movie *A Beautiful Mind*, it completely rocked my world. It is the story of a brilliant mathematician. He has a job that uses his incredible mind, a beautiful supportive wife, and a great best friend whom he had a great time in college with.

Everything in his life is just perfect.

As the movie continues, we watch as his friends discover that things aren't quite as he had led them to believe. It turned out that there actually was no job that he had been going to each day. When they arrived at his supposed place of employment, there were just scribbles all over the walls. Then they found out that there had been no friend in college, etc.

The reality that we had observed was completely in his head. It wasn't real. He had fabricated all of it. He was diagnosed with schizophrenia and soon realized that he couldn't trust his own brain and perception of what was going on around him.

At this point, I was living on the farm, had two little babies, foster kids, and was living a life that was incredibly different than anything I ever could have imagined. But I told myself every day how great it was. How awesome my relationship with my husband was. How healthy it was to live on the farm. How lucky I was to have this life. I told myself this often enough that a certain portion of myself was actually believing it.

But after watching this movie, something was far too familiar. I began looking around me and started wondering if any of it was real. Had I created characters out of the real humans around me? Had I created the image of the perfect husband and simply applied this to mine whether it was true or not? Had I created a fantasy about the farm life? Had I been telling myself stories of Green Acres, fresh air and "the good farm life", but actually been really suffering inside?

I remember looking at my husband and wondering if I had ever met the real man. Initially, I knew that he was really fun and good looking with an awesome sparkle in his eyes. But what else was true about him? What about him had I made up because it was what I wanted. Who was he really?

What about my children? Who were they really? Had I created visions of the ideal children and superimposed them onto the real little people? What about my parents, sisters, friends, in-laws? Had I ever really met any of these people?

I felt like I had created an entire world in my mind that didn't even exist. I felt like I had built personas around those I loved based on what I felt was in their hearts and what I imagined their potential was.

Now, perhaps we do this with children. We sense what they are good at. We imagine their potential which helps us create the space for them to achieve it. It's not a bad thing. It's natural.

Unless what we are imagining isn't actually true and we are not even interacting with the real person - only a fantasy version of them.

In the Taoist philosophy, there is a teaching about understanding the nature of the animal. In the book *The Tao of Pooh* by Benjamin Hoff (one of my favourite books), they describe each character in the same way we might describe the people in our lives. There is Owl who is always pontificating and telling you things you should know about. There is Piglet who is afraid of everything. There is Rabbit who never stops working and thinks you should do the same. There is Tigger who is always light and carefree and doesn't care about anything except bouncing.

When we look at the people around us and we simply recognize who they are, without trying to project onto them what we want or hope them to be, then we are actually interacting with that person - not a made-up version of them.

This benefits us because we don't waste time and energy being upset and frustrated with someone who isn't doing what we want but is actually totally acting within their nature. And it benefits them because they don't have to pretend to be something they're not just to make us happy and they are truly seen and loved for who they are.

FINDING JOY IN ALL SITUATIONS

We are often taught to always find joy. That our inner happiness should not dependent on our external circumstances. That we need to simply change our viewpoint and what we see will change.

Very often, this is exactly the perfect teaching. When we are in a situation that is difficult and we stay very focused on everything that is wrong, not only will we have a horrible existence in that experience, we will not be able to think clearly or find solutions because we are so emotionally triggered by everything that's happening.

Sometimes we have been raised in homes that saw the negative in everything. We may learn to focus on everything that is horrible in the world and miss everything that is wonderful. In this case, it is really important to find the good in situations.

Also, when we only see the negative, we can become very reactive in stressful situations. Our fears put us in fight-or-flight mode which not only tends to escalate the situation, we are unable to find a good solution, we don't learn anything and we are doomed to repeat it over and over again.

Instead, if we seek to find the quiet inside the storm, we will have a very different experience. When we are still inside, we will be able to see the characters for who they really are. Under the person screaming, we will see the hurt child. Under the person being ultra-defensive, we see someone struggling to have their voice heard. And sometimes we simply see people acting in old patterns that they don't realize aren't the only way through.

From this place, we don't need judgement and we don't need to add to the chaos. We can take what we need. We can ask for guidance to perhaps heal the situation. We can even see the chaos for being a wonderful thing. We are alive. We are interacting. It's all good.

SOMETIMES THIS WORKS AGAINST US

But this does not mean that we should stay in a difficult situation forever.

If we are in an abusive relationship, there is a time when we need to sit quietly, pray and ask for guidance. Maybe we are there for a reason.

Maybe we are both there to learn something important - and this won't come the easy way. During this time, it is important to always find the calm in the storm and see if there is a healing way through.

However, there is a point where we realize that nothing is going to change. This is the situation and the other person has no interest in making it any different. This is simply who they are. This is when we know that the time for finding the calm centre and focusing on the positive is likely over. It is likely time for a change.

This is where our own personal truth must come first.

WHY ARE WE THE ONLY ONES WHO CAN BE UPSET?

One of the reasons I keep the peace is because I don't want anyone to be upset.

The weird thing is that it isn't that I don't want *anyone* to be upset. Just *other* people. If *I* am upset, this seems to be fine. I've never wanted anyone to be mad at me. But it's okay if I'm quietly mad at them. I don't want to hurt anyone's feelings. But it's okay if they hurt my feelings.

I remember counselling a man once who was struggling to be honest with his wife. After telling me everything that was going wrong and everything that his wife was doing that was really upsetting him, I asked him if he had mentioned anything to her.

He replied, "No, I don't want to cause any trouble."

The problem is that there *is* trouble. There is meanness and a lack of connection. There are feelings being hurt - intentionally and unintentionally. There are unsaid things that are screaming in the darkness.

He wasn't *causing* trouble. He was simply saying out loud what was going on.

It is the same with us. If we are upset, then we are simply stating that we are upset. We aren't causing trouble. We aren't creating a problem. A problem already exists. We are simply calling it out.

ALLOWING OURSELVES TO BE ANGRY

After a lifetime of trying not to be angry, I have come to realize that anger is an important part of not getting walked on in life.

We are often taught that there is something wrong with anger. That it is a sign of weakness, bitchiness, or being a difficult person. Plus, anger has gotten a bad rap because it is often confused with rage and temper tantrums.

So let's first understand what rage and temper tantrums are.

When someone (a full grown adult or a 2-year-old) starts screaming "in anger" at another person, this is likely a temper tantrum. They are screaming for attention either to get their own way or to scare and intimidate whomever they are yelling at.

For many people, this display of a loss of control has worked for them to get their own way for their whole life. Simply crying wouldn't have gotten them what they wanted. But if they screamed and got really angry, eventually the other person would cave in and they would get their way.

These kinds of tantrums are often seen in adults when they "lose their minds" on their children - screaming at them for something the child has done. It can also be partners screaming horrible things at each other during a fight. They are fully aware of the fact that they are being unreasonable because they are being unreasonable on purpose. This is the point - to be so over-the-top that they win the battle.

The key difference between this and rage is that during a tantrum, they are fully conscious of what they are doing. However, during rage, the person is truly "seeing black" and has totally lost control of themselves.

This kind of rage only happens in certain people. But when it does, it's like everything goes dark, the world disappears and they just "count the bodies" after it has passed. They barely remember what happened. And if they do, they will say that they had no control over themselves. Often, they won't even remember it. They will continue on in their day like nothing happened and they won't understand why you are so upset.

Both blind rage and manipulative temper tantrums are not anger. They are both dysfunctional results of pain, unconsciousness, and unresolved issues. The rage is never controlled and the temper tantrums have simply always worked. Both are extremely unhealthy with very negative repercussions for everyone involved.

HEALTHY ANGER

Anger is a natural emotion that simply protects us from being walked on. Anger rises when our personal self-protection mechanisms get triggered because someone is physically, emotionally, mentally or spiritually harming us.

We all know that feeling. Someone says something rude or inappropriate and our blood starts to boil. This is an appropriate response. If someone hits you and anger rises to protect yourself, this is an appropriate response. If someone is manipulating you spiritually or emotionally using all kinds of slick words and guilt trips, something in you will say "Don't listen to them. Walk away." This is an appropriate response.

It is the strength of this emotion that helps us stand our ground. It's like our natural adrenaline that keeps things in check until they are resolved.

The problem is that we either don't allow ourselves to feel this anger in the first place or we quickly get rid of it and the problem repeats itself over and over again.

I have done this a lot in my life.

I once had a narcissistic business partner whom I was angry with all the time. But I kept it inside. I didn't want to upset him and rock the boat. I judged myself for feeling anger. I felt like I was above that. And to make it worse, there is a common spiritual idea that says - "obviously what you are seeing in him is really about you". The misunderstanding of this idea has allowed more people-pleasers to be walked on than any other spiritual idea.

I definitely did it in my marriage. If I was angry or hurt, I would try to say something and it wouldn't go well leaving me not knowing what to do with my anger. So, I would meditate, go for a walk or eat some chocolate. I did whatever it would take to not be angry anymore. There was no point. And truthfully, I didn't like the feeling of being angry. It was upsetting and not what I believed my natural state to be.

However, this also meant that issues seldom got resolved. We repeated many of the same patterns over and over again. So, after 20 years, why did we split? Well, many of these unresolved issues were definitely part of it.

I often wonder what would have happened if I had allowed myself to stay angry. What if I had used the strength of that anger and stood my ground until the situations were resolved? Would things have turned out differently? Would we have still gotten divorced? Or would we have split even sooner?

I don't know. At the time, leaving was not an option for me. So, I swallowed my anger, stayed quiet and desperately hoped that time would simply heal our issues.

I don't blame my ex-husband for any of this. By swallowing my anger, I wasn't being honest with him. He had no idea just how upset I was. If I had acted truthfully, my anger could have had a healthy role to play in our relationship.

It was me who wasn't honouring it.

Chapter 12

Your Truth Always Matters

I was recently in a relationship where it was the first time I've ever felt what it was like to be totally honest with a man.

As we got closer and got more involved in each other's lives, thoughts and the way we saw the world, one night I found myself quite angry with him. My normal response would have been to swallow it, to understand that I had a part to play in this. It wasn't all his stuff. It was best to just let it go.

Well, about two weeks earlier, I had a feather tattooed onto my left forearm. For me, it represented mastery - a goal that I believe we are all meant to be aiming for in this new world. Afterwards, I visited my 75-year-old Irish friend who is normally quite the atheist. When I showed her my tattoo, she said, "Did you know that in some Native cultures, when a person holds an eagle feather, they must always tell the truth?"

I looked down at the eagle feather now permanently tattooed onto my arm. *Crap*. Well this definitely changed things. I was going to have to be honest all of the time.

It's not that I was a manipulative liar or something before. It wasn't like that. I just liked to tell *soft* truths. I liked to avoid conflict and pretend that things were okay even when they weren't. I liked to tell just enough of the truth to get the point across but leave out anything that might cause hard feelings.

Perhaps I felt that I was just being polite and not rocking a boat that didn't have to be rocked.

So, here I found myself quite annoyed with my new man. I was about to tell him what I was upset about and then I saw the feather out of the corner of my eye.

I instantly realized that what I was going to say wasn't really the truth. It was a version of the truth. It was a digestible version of the truth. It was a safe version of the truth. It turns out that I am very creative and can come up with all kinds of things so that I don't have to say what the actual simple truth is.

So I sat with it and I asked myself what the truth really was. And I couldn't find it. It was like the half-truth that I was wanting to say to him was the same thing I had convinced *myself* of. I was so attached to what I *wanted* to be true, that I was completely deceiving *myself* as to what the actual truth really was.

And so, I had to dig deeper into myself.

What was this truth that I was afraid to say? What was the truth that I didn't want to hear?

Then suddenly I heard it. I realized that sharing this truth could mean the end of our relationship. I sadly realized that we didn't have a middle ground on this topic. I really didn't like his perspective and sugar-coating it would simply have been a lie.

And I had this eagle feather staring at me. I had no choice.

So I shared my actual truth. It wasn't mean or insulting. It was just my perspective.

And it definitely began an argument. He felt triggered and ganged up on. He continued to argue. But I held my ground.

At one point, I even yelled at him (this was new). He told me that he didn't want me to be angry. Something new rose up inside of me and I said, "I am allowed to be angry. I am allowed to feel however I want! If you don't want me to be angry, stop saying things that piss me off!"

Hmmm... That was interesting.

And then we fell quiet and stared off into the distance. The interesting thing is that neither of us were fighters and we actually really loved each other. There was absolutely no joy in fighting.

Then he quietly said, "Thank you for talking to me about this. I've never actually talked about it with anyone. I understand what you're saying. You're right. I'll work on fixing it."

What? Being honest worked? Conflict didn't destroy me? Or us?

After this, I noticed so many times when I previously would have told only 70% of the truth - avoiding all of the uncomfortable stuff. But now, instead of sharing the partial truth, I would sit quietly, listen within, and wait until I heard the whole 100%.

And whether I liked it or not, the other 30% had to come out eventually. There is a whole truth that has to be shared. So I really had to ask myself why was I dragging out the process. Why was I putting off the inevitable?

I think sometimes I hoped that the whole thing would just fix itself without me having to share that last dreaded 30%.

Maybe the other person would shift or change. Maybe the relationship would even end before I had to share it.

I had to realize that that last 30% wasn't judgement about the other person. It was simply the rest of my truth.

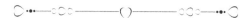

TRYING NOT TO BE JUDGEMENTAL

Some of my challenge was that I truly believe that it is best not to judge others. I have always tried to give people the benefit of the doubt. I don't want people to judge me, so I've always tried not to judge them.

There is obviously a beautiful teaching here. To literally sit in judgement of someone else is just not okay. To decide someone's worth or whether they are making the right or wrong decision is simply none of our business. To decide that someone is a good or bad person assumes that we are somehow above them and are qualified to make such a decision about another human being.

Obviously, learning not to judge is an excellent teaching. But this can really work against us because we are deleting important information in our interactions with others. And when we do this, it is generally us who will get the short end of that stick.

JUDGEMENT VS OPINION

I would have a very specific discussion with my step-mother often. She would tell me what she thought of another person. They could be anything from amazing to a pain in her ass.

I would argue with her that she shouldn't be so judgemental. And she would look at me like I was a starry-eyed, naive child and say, "Oh for god's sake Katrina, it's not a judgement. It's just the way it is."

In my time on the island, I had to seriously rethink my step-mother's perspective here. Maybe she was right. Maybe "calling a spade a spade" isn't a judgement, it is simply an observation. And perhaps, these observations are what keep us safe and around the kinds of people that we want to be around.

For example, in the wild, if we observed another animal acting in an aggressive, dangerous way, it is in our best interest to recognize this behaviour and log it in our minds. This way, we will avoid them or at least be ready to run if needed.

However, if we were to apply our "do not judge" law on this, then we are suddenly not allowed to register our observation. We must withhold judgement on the other creature... and of course, risk being eaten.

So then what is the difference between an opinion and a judgement?

A judgement decides whether someone or something is right or wrong or good or bad. It is a judgement - like in a court of law.

This is different than having an opinion or perceiving another person's characteristics.

While on the island, I was reading Agatha Christie's autobiography. What struck me the most (besides how amazed I was that she could make me fascinated by her thoughts as a 4-year-old) was how she characterized all of the people in her life. She simply observed and categorized them in a way that I, for some reason, was not allowed to. If I said the things she said, I would have considered myself judgemental. Yet, when I read Agatha, it was simply refreshing and... well... simple.

The difference between Agatha and myself was pretty drastic.

Let's say I met a young man who was abrasive and rude. Here is an example of my inner dialogue. I would initially assume that he's a nice guy underneath his tough exterior. He obviously had a difficult childhood where he was demeaned and made to feel inadequate. So, I should try extra hard with him because he simply hasn't had the love that I've had in my life and he lacks the communication skills to connect with others. After all, everyone wants true connection. It's human nature. Putting a little extra effort into him is really the kindest thing that I can do.

However, Agatha's description would likely be very different. I imagine that she might say, "Ah yes, Charles was a curious sort. The moment you met him, he always found some way to insult you, perhaps to assert a false sense of power over you and intimidate you. Of course, it was terribly obvious to anyone that he lacked any sense of self-worth and therefore, I found him terribly tiresome and avoided him at all costs."

Now, perhaps there is a time for both perspectives. Maybe there are times when giving a little extra to someone who is obviously struggling is truly the kindest thing to do and maybe it brings us joy to do it. But maybe there are also times to allow ourselves to observe the "nature of the beast" and allow them to just be who they are. Then, we can make decisions based on that.

WHY ARE WE NOT ALLOWED AN OPINION?

Isn't it strange that we do not allow ourselves to have an opinion?

Now, to say that I don't have any opinions is a ridiculous statement. I am very opinionated on many, many topics. However, it is in personal relationships, that things get murky. Even here, I still do have opinions. If someone were to ask me to describe my children, friends, boyfriend, ex-husband, ex-inlaws, etc, I'm quite sure my opinions - positive or negative - would shine through. This isn't where we don't have opinions.

It is when we feel obligated to act in a certain way based on some ideal that we have in our minds. Like the belief that we must tolerate someone being unkind to us because they are an elder, parent, teacher, boss, child, old friend, neighbour, grandparent, etc. This problem only arises where there is a training of some sort that has predefined how you are allowed to act or react to someone.

There are institutions that we are aware of. We are told that there are acceptable ways to act in marriage or how to act within the family/clan. Or the proper way to behave in public. There are rules here and even if we don't consciously believe in them, they are often woven into our consciousness simply by what we learn from discussions around the kitchen table, what we watch on TV or the subtle messages we receive from movies, the news or social media.

LOSING A PART OF US

In the pursuit of not being judgemental, we can lose a sense of who we are.

I can understand the joy of floating neutrality - of not responding to our environment - living in pure non-judgement. But it just isn't complete. If we simply choose to not have an opinion about a situation, we may stay too long in relationships and put up with behaviour that we really should escape.

This often applies to people who were abused as children. No child wants to judge their parents. Children want to be loved and want to love their parents. Therefore, while any abuse is happening, an inner mechanism tries to delete what is going on in the hope that one day it won't be happening and they will actually feel the love that they need from these humans that they love the most.

However, in order to delete what is really happening in order to stay sane and convince themselves that they are loved, they must separate from their inner truth. The part of themselves that is in pain and suffering must be ignored. The opinion that what is happening is wrong or that their parents are actually cruel people must keep quiet or else how can they keep our desire to be loved by these people alive?

But unfortunately, this pattern of separating what is happening to us from our inner truth continues on into the rest of our lives.

It isn't just that we will continue to have abusive partners, bosses and even friends in our lives. The difficult part is that we have stopped having an opinion or judgement about how they are treating us. We are looking at the bright side. We are trying to see the good in people. But most of all, we are used to separating that part of us that is in pain from our current reality from the part of us that just wants to be loved and not have any trouble.

Imagine the difference inside a child's (or adult's) mind if they say to themselves "my dad is a child abuser" versus "my dad has bad days and loses control". The first is clear and actually describes what is going on and puts the responsibility in the hands of the father. But in the second case, it isn't clear. The child may continue the inner thoughts to include "I have to be better and not cause trouble." or "It's because I'm not good enough. I'm not a good enough daughter/son/person. He's like this because of me."

The other problem is that because we are not connected to that strong opinion that "calls a spade a spade", it is much harder to change our situation. We will feel powerless because we actually have no sense of self within the situation. We know that we don't like being treated this way and sometimes we know that something is wrong enough to complain to our friends that our partner is a jerk or abusive or that we had a crappy childhood. But it just doesn't connect anywhere solid inside. We have long lost touch with who we are and what our opinions are on these kinds of subjects.

CHAPTER 13

FOLLOWING OUR INNER TRUTH

I remember chatting with a woman one day, while getting a facial in Toronto.

She had been dating this guy that she met in a dance club. He had danced with her, kissed her and wooed her all night. She was totally infatuated. He messaged her for a few days and then communication slowed way down. She tried to question him but he always had an excuse. He told her that she was being needy. That she was smothering him. He even tried to tell her that obviously she was like this because of past relationships and that she was just projecting past behaviour onto him.

This went on for a while. When they went dancing again, he acted as if he wasn't there with her. He was distant and strange. Yet, he continued to argue with her that it was all in her head, that she was just being overly sensitive and needy.

In the end, she found out that he was married. Her instincts had been right all along.

So why didn't she listen? Why didn't she just trust her instincts when she knew something was wrong?

Why didn't she trust her inner truth?

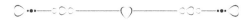

WHAT DOES YOUR STOMACH WANT?

My son is a born people-pleaser. Even as a small child, when I would ask him if he wanted to do something, you could see him pause and "scan" me to see what the answer was that I wanted. Then, he would tell me what he thought would make me happy.

He was 4-years-old when I was going through my healing experience with the breast lumps. At this time, I was learning to listen to my own truth and to stop scanning others for what they wanted me to say.

So, when I saw this behaviour in him, I definitely didn't want him doing it either.

Well, we often have some place of weakness in our bodies that will flare up when we are stressed out. For my son, it was his stomach. He was often bullied at school and never said anything to us. But I would always know that something was up when he would wake up with a stomach ache and not want to go to school.

So, I would let him stay home from school. As we worked around the farm together, eventually he would share what was bothering him. But his stomach was always the key.

So I began using his sensitive stomach to help him share his truth. When I would ask him a question and I saw him begin his "people-pleasing scan", I would ask him "What does your stomach want? Does your *stomach* want to do it?"

Inevitably, he would say, "Oh no, my stomach does not want to do that." And the truth would have been found.

TRUSTING OUR INTUITION

At one point in my travels, there was a lot of drama happening in the family I was staying with. It was about the family business, the father-in-law, and money. Tensions were high with lots of yelling and arguing. My hostess/friend in particular was very stressed out because the difficult conversations between the warring parties were all falling on her shoulders. She was so stressed out and on the verge of tears.

That afternoon, she had to go into town to take her daughters to their lessons and sports. She asked me if I would like to go with her. They would be about six hours in the city.

Well, there wasn't a bone in my body that wanted to go into town that day. I was deep in my writing and emotionally, I just didn't want to be around the situation.

But she could really use a friend. I really should go and give her someone to talk to about all of this.

Plus, I was having my own low day. Sometimes it's exhausting to be immersed in a language that you don't understand. Plus, hearing people yelling at each other all of the time was really getting to me. So much yelling. So much drama.

And now I was feeling really obligated to go to town and be a good friend.

Hmmm…

So I went to my little room and meditated. I sat on my bed, put on headphones, listened to some soothing yoga music and breathed deeply.

What was the answer?
    Stay home.
But she's my friend.
    Stay home.
But she's upset.
    So are you.
But…

The bottom line was that I had to decide whether listening to my heart was the right thing or not. So, I stayed home and trusted that it was the right decision.

Six hours later, everyone arrived home and my friend was all smiles.

"Did you do something Katrina?" she said with a big smile on her face.

"What do you mean?"

"The whole problem has been resolved. It makes no sense. My father-in-law called the other man and fixed everything. It's just not possible. I think you must have sent a spirit or something to fix it!"

I just stared at her. She was beaming. She was so happy.

Staying home was absolutely the best thing I could have done for everyone.

FINDING TRUE SELF-LOVE

CHAPTER 14

TRUE SELF-LOVE

One day, during my travels, I was quite frustrated with a man who liked to visit the family I was staying with. It seemed like he was forever yelling and berating everyone. We would be sitting just having a nice time playing cards or chatting, he would walk into the room, start yelling at someone, and instantly the whole room would become quiet. The mood changed instantly from nice and easy to tense and depressing.

I witnessed this over and over again. Other people would come over and within ten minutes, he would be lecturing the new person about something. It was just annoying me so much!

At one point, I sat back and asked myself why this man annoyed me so much. Maybe he had a bad attitude. Maybe he had a temper. But why was he particularly hitting *my* buttons. Why was I taking everything personally - especially when he was never doing it to me!

The truth was that he sounded just like the critical voice inside my own head - the voice that says that people won't like what I write. That people won't like me once they get to know me. That I am too much. That it's best to just assume that things won't work out so that I'm not disappointed.

Yes, this voice in my head was just like this guy. It was relentless and every day, there was a certain part of my consciousness whose job it was to quieten it and keep it happy.

Once I realized this, I just wanted to delete it from my mind. I wanted to get rid of this negativity. But how?

I called a friend and asked him if he thought this was even possible. Could I actually delete this negative thought pattern from my brain?

My wise friend said, "No, it's a part of you. You can't delete it. Instead, you need to go deeper to find what's underneath it. Stay in the swamp my friend. You'll find the answer."

Hmmm. OK.

So that night, I lay in bed and asked, "What is under this critical voice?"

The answer came. And I cried.

It was a little girl. It was a little girl who didn't get invited to the birthday party. It was a little girl who didn't understand the world. She didn't understand why it was cool to be bad. She didn't understand why it was wrong to try hard in school or why it was wrong to be nice to teachers. She didn't have this rebel desire. She just wanted to be herself. But slowly she was realizing that if she was just herself, the other kids would make fun of her and she would be alone. Who she was was somehow wrong. She didn't fit in. She was an outsider.

Oh how I cried for my little girl. I was instantly seven years old and feeling everything that my little self felt.

This was why this critical/protective voice was born. This voice took care of my little girl by telling her that other people didn't matter. They just didn't understand. There was no point hoping they will like you because they won't. Other people won't understand what you like to do so just don't tell them. Keep your truth a secret. It's better this way.

This way we won't be disappointed.

Suddenly a million memories started flooding into me. Memories of things I had done that my little girl absolutely didn't want to do. I was crying and my body was shaking and I was so hot inside. But I just let it flow and decided to write my little girl a letter.

Here is what it said:

> *I'm so sorry. I love you. I'm so sorry. I'm here now.*
> *I can't believe how often I made you have sex when*
> *you didn't want to. I'm so sorry.*
> *I'm sorry for all the diets I went on because they said*
> *there was something wrong with us.*
> *I'm sorry for every moment I've looked at myself in*
> *disgust of the fat or cellulite or the shape of my breasts.*
> *I'm sorry for making you exercise to the point of pain and*
> *still thinking that there was something wrong with us.*
> *I'm sorry for working you into the ground.*
> *I'm sorry for putting you in uncomfortable situations*
> *because my pride said we were strong enough.*
> *I'm sorry for not speaking up for you when you didn't*
> *like what was happening.*
> *I'm sorry for not honouring your love of romance and*
> *settling for so much less.*
> *I'm sorry for stressing you out when all I had to do was*
> *trust.*
> *I'm sorry for not letting you cry.*

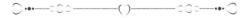

BEING A BEACON OF LOVE

Years ago, I had asked my first teacher, Jim, what I was supposed to be doing with my life. What was my career supposed to be?

He replied, "You are meant to be a beacon of love in the world."

What? This was not the answer that I was looking for. I wanted a meaningful job that paid the bills and made me happy. I had no interest in being a beacon of love. I wanted a real answer.

But now, more than 20 years later, as I headed out into the world on my new adventure, his words came flooding back to me. So much so, that I had a heart tattooed on my arm, so that I would remember what my "role" was.

BACK ON THE ISLAND...

But here, I was failing. I was struggling to love them. I could love them as human beings. But my judgement was definitely in overdrive and I really didn't like them. So, to say I loved them was definitely not true.

One night, as I lay in bed struggling with my feelings of failure, wondering if they were mad at me, the lack of connection and why I was even there, something dawned on me. I had this whole "beacon of love" idea wrong. I was supposed to be loving *me*. It wasn't about loving others.

Jim would never have recommended that I take on some kind of Messiah complex. I had totally misinterpreted what he had said. He never believed in saving others. He believed that each person was connected to God and each of us just had to walk our own paths. He believed that all of this saviour stuff was just an ego-trip.

I couldn't believe it took me twenty years to figure out what he had actually said.

I needed to love *me*. I needed to make choices based on what was the most loving for *me*. And then, when I am filled with overflowing love, that love and kindness effortlessly spreads to others.

WHAT IS SELF-LOVE?

Finding self-love is no small thing. And I think the problem is that we are looking in all the wrong places. We think that it is looking in the mirror and telling ourselves an uplifting mantra. But that doesn't work or we wouldn't still be talking about it.

What was it really for me?

It was choosing my own happiness over the perceived discomfort of another.

It was looking deeply into my own pain from childhood and acknowledging my inner child and choosing to love and listen to her every day with the goal of fully integrating her again.

It was honouring my truth and no longer eating eyeballs. It was realizing that my truth was more than just my opinion or my preference. It was exactly how this soul responds to the world it's living in. It is the truth of my soul. This is nothing to ignore.

It was believing in my perception of the world. Although the world seems to be so full of anger and hate and it seems so hopeless, I have always believed that there was real perfection in it, whether we could see it or not.

I have always felt a strong connection to God and although it is not the popular belief with many people, this is my truth. I have been accused of being naive, silly and crazy for sitting in silence waiting for guidance. And yet, when I wait, and I follow, such amazing things always happen - things that I could never have expected.

Honouring my beliefs about the world is the ultimate way that I can be loving to myself. Because within this world, I also get to follow my intuition, regardless of the thoughts of others. I get to stand in my truth and assume that it is important that I do it for some reason.

Self-love is just letting ourselves be our whole self. Full intuition listening. Full truth all of the time.

This is true self-love.

CHAPTER 15

SOMETIMES YOU MUST LEAVE

And sometimes they won't understand.

After seven weeks, I decided to leave the island early. It was a decision that tormented me because I hated to not fulfill my commitment and I didn't want to disappoint my hosts.

But it also bothered me that I knew that they wouldn't understand. The very reason that I felt so alone, isolated and despondent was the fact that they didn't emotionally connect with me. There was no way I was going to be able to explain it to them.

In their own way, they had been very kind. They had paid for everything. I had my own room and bathroom. They had been willing to buy me anything I needed.

But what I really needed was friendship, empathy and human connection.

So, now I had to tell her that I was leaving three weeks early. I was going to disappoint her. She wouldn't be happy. I really didn't want to do this. And yet, I absolutely had to.

Maybe she would be relieved. Maybe the experience wasn't what *she* had hoped for either. Maybe I was doing us both a big favour here. I was hopeful that this was the case. But deep down I knew that this wasn't how it was going to play out.

OK. I was ready. My hostess was out on the porch. I would tell her now.

As I walked out, I saw her standing by the table with a bowl of something in front of her. As I sat down, I saw that there were three langouste in the bowl (a relative of the lobster). The langouste were crawling around obviously trying to escape.

As I took a deep breath to tell her what I needed to say, she began breaking off the legs of the little creatures. As they crawled around, she just kept breaking their legs off. Oh my god, it was so upsetting. I am a total animal lover – whether they are furry or covered in a shell.

And then she took a knife and started trying to kill them by stabbing them.

I honestly looked to the heavens and asked, *"Really? I have to tell her while she is killing little creatures? Am I being tested?"*

And so, I took a deep breath and kept going.

Because of the language barrier, I tried to keep my words simple. I told her that I needed to change my flights to fly out this coming Saturday. I told her that I was lonely and needed to return to Canada for a while.

She gave me an annoyed look and said, "You will be lonely in Canada too."

Hmm. So she's not relieved. Damn.

I told her that I was struggling not understanding the language. She replied that I should have gotten out more and met more people so that I could practice my French. *What? I should have left the family to go and do my own thing?* This just wasn't computing.

She looked at me and decided that it definitely wasn't the language problem. It was because I had a boyfriend back in Canada. There was no way that I could be away from him this long. *This* was really the problem.

Of course, none of this was true. She didn't understand me at all. She couldn't understand what it was like to connect in the way I was accustomed to. It just wasn't her.

I simply had to leave anyway. Even if she would never understand.

○••—○○○ ———— ( ) ———— ○○○—••○

BUT WHAT IF THEY ARE NICE TO US?

Well, the test didn't end there. After I said this to her, I left the porch because I couldn't stomach watching her massacre the creatures any longer. As I sat in the living room chatting with my sister on the phone, she came in and offered me a drink. "Here, I made you a rum punch," she said with a big smile.

Huh? Wasn't she upset? Was she just being nice to me because I was upset? What was going on?

Maybe she's feeling badly for everything? Was she changing her ways? Was I just meant to be honest so that things would change? Should I stay now?

Crap. It was easier when she was ignoring me. Now what should I do?

Then she told me that the next day was a holiday and that they would be taking me to a beautiful island.

What? How could I disappoint them when they were being nice to me now?

THE SEAT WITH A VIEW

Well, we went to one of the most beautiful islands I have ever seen. It was like it had been painted in this raw, perfect way that couldn't possibly be real. But regardless of the beauty surrounding me, I was absolutely miserable inside. I was in total limbo. *Could I really leave? Will they drive me to the airport? Will they be disappointed in me?*

Well, this inner struggle went on until we went out for lunch. We went into a restaurant right on the ocean. We were shown a lovely table with bench seats facing the ocean. One bench faced the ocean and the other faced inside the restaurant.

I thought to myself, "Oh, what a beautiful view. This will be fine." Eating together had become a really difficult time in the day because they always spoke in their language to each other and I just sat there mute not understanding anything. So, I thought that this view would be perfect because I could look at it while they talked amongst themselves.

But then the realization hit me. *They aren't going to give me the seat with the view. They will take it for themselves. Crap.*

So, I hung back a bit to see what they would do. Sure enough, they stood in front of the "seats with a view" so that the 10-year-old and I would have to take the seats with our backs to the ocean.

As I sat down and watched them talk to each other in their language, something quietened inside of me. I realized that these people were nothing like me. Like *nothing* like me. I would *always* have given my visitors the seat with the view. ALWAYS. But it hadn't even crossed their mind. I'm not sure it was ever even a thought.

I realized that I was assuming that I was dealing with people who were like me. I had assumed that they were caring about me in the same way that I cared and thought about them.

But sometimes, it just isn't true.

Sometimes, they take the seat with the view without even considering you.

They'll guilt you into eating eyeballs without considering how uncomfortable and foreign it might be for you.

They let you sit alone mute with their friends and not translate for you. And they don't even notice your discomfort.

Something in this moment changed everything for me.

I no longer felt bad about leaving. In that moment I made my final decision to change my flights that evening. No matter what.

This was the kindest thing that I could do for me.

In fact, it might have been the nicest thing that I had ever done for myself.

CHAPTER 16

GOING HOME

Once we were back home, I changed my flights to fly out a few days later. My hosts drove me to the airport early because they had to work in the morning. So I would wait at the airport for about eight hours before my flight left. But this was good. It gave me lots of time to ponder and be so thankful that I was going home.

There was a happiness inside of me that I couldn't even describe. I had actually made a decision based solely on my own happiness. I had made a hard decision because I wanted to be kind to myself.

I was amazed that I had done it. I had spent my life throwing myself to the wolves in so many ways. Sometimes it was for good causes - like defending someone or speaking before town councils to build skateparks for kids. But most of the time I just didn't consider the effect that these things would have on me, and on my little girl.

But this time, I had done it. I had actually been kind to myself.

I had overridden all of the people-pleasing training, the spiritual ideals that I had held myself to, and my fear of not fulfilling a commitment.

I had chosen *me* for once. I had chosen what would make my little girl happy.

I had actually chosen me.

And it felt truly wonderful.

ACKNOWLEDGEMENTS

I would like to thank my daughter, Taylor Bos, who accompanied me on this "eyeball" writing journey. There were many days through my travels when I just couldn't bring this book together. I thought I could finish this book after leaving the island. But alas, it wouldn't let itself be finished. I was in Italy at the time and her wise advice was to shelve the book and allow more experiences to happen. This was the best advice I could've heard and followed. Truly finding self-love in Italy and a deepened faith in Greece helped me write the book that I truly wanted to write.

Lynn Borth is the wonderful artist who created the cover of my book. It is a challenge and an act of faith to ask an artist to create something from a vision that you can barely see yourself. So, I am thrilled with Lynn's beautiful creation of our friend on the cover who knows that she will not be eating eyeballs anymore.

I would like to thank my friends who gave me their invaluable suggestions and encouragement in the final editing process of this book: Angela Pickering-Peeters, Roula Said, Tanya Bechard, Christel Crawford, Bill Hartman, Carey Adams, Amanda Miller, Kristen Engel, Lisa Boonstoppel-Pot, Emily Marks, Vic Harding, and Shelley Adams.

I would also like to thank everyone I met along my travels who played the characters in my story who inspired me, triggered me, and helped me grow.

About the Author

Katrina Bos is a Canadian speaker, author, and teacher of tantra, meditation, and spiritual studies. She is the founder of Fusion Tantra, an online school where she teaches how to integrate the ancient wisdom of tantra into every aspect of our lives.

In 2018, she gave away everything she owned and headed out into the world on a "Journey of the Mystic" - listening within for each step, deepening her connection, and discovering people, places and experiences that she never could have imagined.

Her first book, "What If You Could Skip the Cancer", is the story of when she met her first teacher, Jim, who helped her begin her true spiritual journey. Her second book, "Tantric Intimacy", shares stories and teachings to help us integrate the wisdom of tantra into every aspect of our lives.

She is based out of Toronto, Canada and is currently travelling, exploring, writing, and teaching around the world.

For more information, please see her websites: www.katrinabos.ca and www.fusiontantra.com.